hot & hip GRILLING SECRETS

A Fresh Look at Cooking with Fire

WRITTEN AND PHOTOGRAPHED BY
BONNIE MATTHEWS

Skyhorse Publishing

Skyhorse Publishing books may be purchased in bulk at special discounts for sales promotion, corporate gifts, fund-raising, or educational purposes. Special editions can also be created to specifications. For details, contact the Special Sales Department, Skyhorse Publishing, 307 West 36th Street, 11th Floor, New York, NY 10018 or info@skyhorsepublishing.com.

Skyhorse® and Skyhorse Publishing® are registered trademarks of Skyhorse Publishing, Inc.®, a Delaware corporation.

Visit our website at www.skyhorsepublishing.com.

10 9 8 7 6 5 4 3 2 1

Library of Congress Cataloging-in-Publication Data is available on file.

Cover photo by Bonnie Matthews
End paper illustrations by Bonnie Matthews

Print ISBN: 978-1-63220-292-5
Ebook ISBN: 978-1-63220-753-1

Printed in China

Contents

For all my Facebook friends who follow me at "Bonnie On Oz" who have been with me on this journey of inspiring others about healthy food and mindful living.

And to Cremora, my cat and companion who was ever present during the photo shoots and patiently awaited leftovers after the shots.

Special thanks to Alysia Gadson, my friend and neighbor who lent me her grill and tasted all the recipes with me. Her feedback was invaluable. And thanks for sneaking in my apartment and doing the dishes! You're a real gem!

Also to my friends, Arabella Girardi, Emily Duke, and Kelli Felix who assisted with writing, photo shoots, and taste testing!

To Bloodroot Blades for providing their amazing hand crafted knife for one of the shots; and to Black Diamond Meats for providing premium grass-fed beef and pork for some of the recipes. Also to Maya and Richard for allowing me to chill and shoot some of the photos at their airbnb.com hideaway spot in Ojai, California.

Introduction

A Fresh Look at Cooking with Fire

It's unmistakable—that wonderful smell of someone grilling in summer! That smell of charcoal brings up so many memories of impromptu neighborhood gatherings. It's a ritual—everyone dusts off the patio furniture that first warm day in summer and heads to the store to get hotdogs, burgers, and coleslaw. Am I right?

Grilling is naturally a great way to entertain, since everyone can gather on a back patio. There's something about a fire that brings people together. Socializing, sharing food, Frisbee throwing, and cooking, all at once. That works for me! It's a time to slow down and connect with our neighbors and friends without the TV or Internet—and it gets people outside. What's more, everyone participates so you, as the host, aren't stuck in the kitchen doing all the work. It's a given that if you show up for a grilling party you're going to have fun.

Bacon is all the rage these days—but you won't find pork bacon in this book. You also won't find blue cheese burgers, bones, skin, or beer cans up the butt of a chicken. Yep, there's plenty of those books out there if that's what you are looking for. But I wanted to create something a bit different with *Hot & Hip Grilling Secrets*. I'm integrating a fresher, healthier look at cooking on the grill.

I want to ignite your senses with a new way of thinking about grilling. Instead of the humdrum burger and bun for dinner, I want to share ways to save time and help you meal plan with the leftovers. For example, if you stoke up the grill you may as well cook a whole filet of salmon so you can enjoy part of it right away and the rest on top of a fresh salad for lunch the next day.

This book covers more than grilling meats—you'll learn about grilling fish, veggies, flatbreads, and even baked goods. (Yes, you can bake on the grill! In the heat of summer, who wants to be stuck inside with the oven on? Seriously?) You know that midsummer has arrived when the garden is so overgrown with tomatoes, zucchini, and basil that you don't know what to do with them all. I want to elevate your meals with flavor combinations that will inspire you to use all of them! I'm also going to encourage you to try ingredients you may not be familiar with, like spaghetti squash, that vegetable that you keep passing by at the grocery store because you have no idea how to cook it; it's so versatile and a great substitute for pasta. My focus throughout this book is on fresh, healthy, creative—and delicious—grilling.

There are a few secrets I'm going to share with you that will transform your grilling forever. You'll learn how to craft the right combination of spiciness, sweetness, and tangy vinegar, and just how long to marinate before firing up that grill. And for those folks who steer away from cooking fish on the grill because it always turns out too dry, let me introduce you to the plank! Yes, wood planks when soaked in water create a wonderful base for grilling moist fish filets every time. Planks not only create a moisture barrier and add flavor infused from the wood, they also work as a platter for serving and make for easy clean up. I have more secrets where those came from, so keep reading!

What kind of grill works best?

A giant stainless steel gas grill the size of an Airstream trailer is gorgeous, but not really necessary to create good grilled meals. A standard gas grill or even a simple, inexpensive charcoal kettle grill is truly all you need. I'd steer clear of hibachi-style grills, however, as they seem to lose their heat very quickly because they are so shallow.

The recipes in this book can be made on either a gas grill or a charcoal grill—whichever you prefer. Gas grills are tidy, and they clean and heat up very quickly so they have a nice appeal. Another benefit of gas grills is the ability to maintain an even temperature since you can control the flame. On the other hand, if you can handle a little dirt and smoke, there's nothing better than the taste that a charcoal grill can provide. That extra char and smoky flavor is just so delicious!

My number one grilling secret: A digital temperature gauge!

The temperature gauge is essential for grilling meats, fish, and poultry to avoid overcooking or undercooking. The temperature gauge is essentially a thermometer that you insert in the thickest portion of the meat while it's cooking so you can check to see if the meat is done. Simple! It's important to note that with both gas grills and charcoal grills, not every surface area will have the same temperature. With this tool, you'll be able to check every piece of meat several times on the grill as you move it around. Some pieces of meat will be done sooner than others and can be removed from the grill and set aside, while the others continue to cook.

The Gas Grill—ignite with the flick of a switch and voila!

The gas grill provides a fairly uniform heat source by using a propane tank or natural gas hookup. The propane tanks are easy to hook up and are replaceable. Some gas grills have a separate burner area on the side for cooking side dishes or other items for your meal. Additionally, some gas grills have small counter surface areas that are handy for keeping plates, marinades, and tools (and a glass of wine) while you are cooking!

The Kettle Grill—starts with a match.

Building the fire with hardwood charcoal in your kettle grill starts with a match.

The old standard of using lighter fluid and charcoal briquettes is really a thing of the past. You can find all kinds of all natural hardwood charcoal on the market now. They are formed from oak, hickory, apple wood, and maple and burn at a very high temperature. They burn really clean and for much longer than the old charcoal briquettes that are laced with petroleum and other additives. I highly recommend using a chimney starter (or "charcoal chimney"), which will speed up the time it takes for the wood to get hot. To use one is easy: you fill the base of the metal cylinder with crumpled newspapers and fill the top portion with the wood chunks. Then you place the starter directly on the grill grate and light the newspaper to start it. After a few minutes, when the top charcoal is burning red and the charcoal begins to have grayish ash, you know it's time to start cooking! Use oven mitts and flip the chimney starter over to pour the charcoal into the grill and carefully set the chimney on a fireproofed area on the ground, away from everyone so no one gets burned. Follow safety tips that come with the product. Chimney starters can be found at every hardware store, both in season and off season and found online for about $15–18.

Once the charcoal is in the base of the grill you can spread them out for direct heat grilling so that no matter where food is placed on the cooking grate it should cook fairly evenly. There's also the indirect heating method where you place all the charcoal on one side of the grill, and place a drip pan under the cooking grate. I prefer not fooling with all that—I just cook with direct heat, all evenly spread out.

Unlike the gas grill, charcoal kettle-style grills don't usually have surface areas attached to them, so a small table nearby will be helpful for you to keep items such as marinades, plates, and tools.

Grilling Secrets

Marinating and Flavor Secrets

Vinegar and citrus juices

Vinegar and citrus juices are great acidic ingredients that break down proteins in meats and help make them more tender. Gone are the days of sprinkling everything with MSG. (If you don't know what MSG is—don't even ask!)

Vinegars come in all kinds of varieties, from tart to sweet. Balsamic comes in white, regular aged brown, and even can be found infused with flavors like black cherry. The old standard apple cider vinegar is inexpensive and pairs great with garlic and most any herb you have on hand for a wonderful marinade. Rice vinegar is delicious for dressings as well as marinades for an Asian-style taste. It's slightly sweet and also comes in a sweeter variety called Mirin.

In addition to the vinegars as an acidic component, freshly squeezed citrus juices are also acidic and work great in all kinds of marinades. Citrus adds a brightness to the marinade as well as the finished product, as the skins can be grated as zest or added as a garnish when plating.

Oils

Oils, used for both marinades and cooking, sometimes get a bad rap, but when used sparingly they provide a lot of moisture to meats. Additionally, some oils have health benefits with their good fats—like avocado oil and coconut oils. Use them in marinades and use as a cooking oil spray to help keep food from sticking to the grill grate. Coconut oil is a favorite of mine and comes in both a liquid and a spray. Almond, walnut, and hazelnut oils are also wonderful for adding to dressings to accompany your meals. For Asian-inspired dishes, toasted sesame seed oil is absolutely fabulous. It's great paired with rice vinegar too!

Herbs & Spices

You can create contrasting flavors for marinades with herbs and spices, giving flavors of both heat and sweet. My big secret is to use peppery heat with a little bit of sweet. The contrast between the two provide a wonderful complement to meats, poultry, and fish. I experiment with lots of varieties of hot peppers, like red Fresno chilis, jalapeño, and banana peppers. Add a little sweet using healthier alternatives to table sugar such as coconut sugar, turbinado, or raw sugar. For liquid sweetness, use local honey, grade b maple syrup, or raw agave nectar.

Top 10 Grilling Secrets & Gadgets

Helpful tools and hints to make you achieve absolutely fabulous food

1. Digital Temperature Gauge
An essential tool for any griller—especially for meats poultry and fish. Cooking at the right temperature ensures you will have moist, tender food!

2. Chimney Starter
The best friend to any charcoal kettle grill is the chimney starter. It gets the hardwood charcoal going and allows it to catch fire quickly and evenly so you can get cooking faster!

3. All Natural Hardwood Charcoal
The second best friend to any charcoal kettle grill. Not only does all natural hardwood charcoal have no chemicals or additives, it provides that classic wonderful charcoal flavor we all adore.

4. Grill Grid
A fabulous stainless steel tray that works great for grilling small loose items such as shrimp, chunks of fish, or vegetables. The grill grid also works great to easily transport food from the grill to the table!

5. Fish Cage
The fish cage includes a long handle and a locking mechanism, and allows for flipping fish easily. It works great for fish that has been stuffed and keeps everything contained.

6. Cedar Wood Planks
The very best way to avoid dried out fish is by using a wood plank. After soaking in water first, they are then placed directly on the grill and act as a natural moisture barrier between the fish and the heat source. They also infuse the fish with the wonderful flavor of the wood! Wood planks also come in maple, hickory, and apple wood.Once the fish is done, the plank acts as a beautiful serving tray at the table.

7. Time to Marinate
For successful and flavorful meats and poultry—just a little bit of planning ahead to give your dish time for marinating will make your food taste so much better.

8. Cedar Paper Wraps
Thin sheets of wood cedar act as a fun wrapper for chunks of fish or vegetables! They make fun, delicious parcels of food for parties and also aid in keeping fish extra moist while they infuse that wonderful cedar flavor.

9. Opposites Attract: heat, sweet and vinegar

Elevate the flavors of meats, poultry, fish, and marinades with a wide variety of spicy peppers, vinegars, and sweet elements. Make use of fresh garden herbs for making all kinds of pestos to add to your dishes. They can make a mediocre chicken breast into something magnificent!

10. Quirky Slider Skewers®

These are fantastic long metal skewers that have a sliding mechanism at the handle that you push down to slide the skewered food off and easily on to your plate! Look for them online!

I started cooking with granulated Himalayan pink salt about eight years ago and only recently discovered the salt slabs for use as a cooking surface! Pink salt is one of the purest in the world, found deep within caves that were created 250 million years ago in the Himalayan Mountains. Unlike sea salt which can be contaminated by heavy metals and pollutants, and table salt, which is chemically cleaned and has additives, the pink salt is ultra-pure. It contains up to eighty-four minerals and trace elements and many cultures use it for its health benefits. Himalayan pink salt also has a pleasantly mild flavor.

The pink salt slab can be placed directly on the grill but needs to be heated up slowly so that it doesn't crack. Because the slabs are all natural crystals, they have cracks and veins and can break off when there is a dramatic temperature change. To avoid this, follow these simple guidelines.

- Make sure the slab is dry and at room temperature prior to placing on a heated grill.
- If you are cooking over live coals, set the salt slab on the grill away from the heat source while it heats up. If you are using a gas grill, leave the lid off and start on low heat, gradually increasing to the desired cooking temperature over a 20 minute period to be safe, prior to cooking.
- Select a recipe for cooking on the slab that does not contain a lot of liquid or sauce. The salt will overpower the flavor of the food since there is constant direct contact with the salt source.
- Once you have finished cooking on the slab, simply scrub the cooled surface with a clean abrasive kitchen sponge and water. Do not submerge the slab in water because it is so porous. Instead, place the slab at an angle and work from the top to the bottom with the sponge and small amounts of water. Once you have cleaned the surface, dry it and do not use it again to cook with for at least twenty-four hours to ensure that the moisture in the cracks dries all the way. After cooking on the slab, you will begin to notice dark marbling effects within the surface; this is normal and will continue over time.
- It's naturally antimicrobial, however, I would consider cooking meats and fish fully vs rare on the salt to be safe.

The slab will last you for many years of cooking and can be used directly on a gas stove indoors as well. Just remember to allow it to heat up on low burners inside and gradually increase the flame for the desired surface temperature for cooking!

About the Author

I've enjoyed cooking ever since I was little. I learned about yams as early as first grade and have loved them ever since. I have no culinary degree, but surely two semesters of gourmet cooking in ninth grade counts for something! It was a great class and a fun way to avoid taking a second language. Let's face it, I wasn't the greatest student in high school, but I was really good at art and chopping and stirring. So as luck would have it, I followed those passions and have integrated them here in this book through food styling and photography and creating flavor profiles and textures within the recipes.

I am terrible at following recipes myself—I am a rebel and don't like to follow directions—so I've created recipes that aren't pretentious, with simple instructions that almost anyone can replicate (with maybe a few more complex ones thrown in for hardcore foodies). My recipes are mainly inventions of my own or inspired by a dish I had at a cafe. I used to eat out at ethnic restaurants quite often when I lived in Washington, DC and Baltimore and grew to love strong flavors of spice and tang. I love socializing around food—but it didn't love me. You see, I used to be very obese—even as a young kid. I never really learned how to say no to food especially growing up in my household. My father was an amazing baker and our house was always filled with homemade french toast breakfasts and homemade rolls at dinner. Christmas was the biggest sugarfest known to man. I never learned to just have one or two cookies . . .

I've taught myself how to move my body more and learned how to work out and lift weights—and how to cook healthier. I created a new way to live with food and still enjoy it socially without sacrificing flavor. I learned that food is not only fuel, but truly an integral part of my joy! I dropped 130 pounds not by drinking protein shakes but by eating food. Real. Beautiful. Fresh. Clean FOOD! I truly believe that providing my body with non-processed, non-chemical, non-hormone-laced foods enabled my body to heal from forty-three years of mistreatment. Eating fresh healthy foods literally saved my life. Additionally, foods that don't have additives and preservatives in them simply taste better. I learned to live with smaller amounts of salt and sugar and not feel like I'm depriving myself of flavor at all.

I recently turned fifty-one and moved to southern California. I wanted to live in an area that matched my new healthy lifestyle! A place where farm fresh ingredients were accessible and where I could surround myself with like-minded folks who love the great outdoors for play and for fitness. It's been a great sunny place in which to explore this new chapter in my life. I am excited to continue to discover new farmer's markets up and down the coast and find new trails to blaze! Accompanied, of course, by a little great California wine.

Hopefully you'll have fun learning about some healthier alternatives for ingredient substitutions and add them into your repertoire the way that I did.

Cheers to your health.
Bonnie

Chapter 1

Planks and Slab Cooking

Whole Filet Salmon on Cedar with Sweet Onions and Honey Mustard Glaze

Makes 4 servings (or use the leftovers for the next two pages of recipes!).

An easy, nearly failsafe way to grill a larger filet of salmon is cooking it on a wooden plank. They can be found in most grocery stores seasonally, and most definitely online. I like the cedar one best, but you can find hickory, cherry, and apple wood and they all offer a nice aroma to the fish or whatever you are grilling. Because they need to be soaked in water prior to hitting the grill, they act as a natural barrier to protect the food from overcooking, and they provide an easier way to do a large piece of fish without a lot of attention if you are entertaining.

Even if you are cooking for just one or two people, go ahead and get a larger filet and cook it while the grill is hot. There are a few meal ideas on the following pages for the leftovers! (OR: See pages 4 and 6 for what you can do with the leftovers!)

1 large filet of salmon, with skin left on one side, about 3 lbs or about ½ lb per serving (I used boneless wild caught Keta salmon)

1 cup honey mustard

2 tablespoons honey, maple syrup, or agave nectar

2 teaspoons extra virgin olive oil

2 cloves fresh garlic, smashed and minced

2 teaspoons water

about 1 teaspoon of fresh or dried thyme leaves

½ sweet Vidalia onion, sliced in thin strips

about 2 tablespoons dried cranberries

fresh crushed black pepper, and sea salt or pink salt as desired

Before grilling: Soak the plank by setting it in a sink full of water. Place a bowl of water on top of the wood to keep it submerged. The plank should be soaked between 1–3 hours prior to cooking.

For the sauce: Mix honey mustard, honey, olive oil, garlic, water, thyme, salt, and pepper in a bowl and set aside.

Preheat grill on high with the lid closed.

Remove the plank from water and dry slightly. Spray both sides with cooking spray and place the plank on the grill with the smooth side up. Allow the wood to heat up for about 5 minutes with the grill closed before adding the fish.

Once the plank is heated, carefully spray the surface with cooking spray and place the filet on the wood, skin-side down. Spoon or brush on the sauce and reduce heat to medium-high. Add the onions and cranberries evenly over the top of fish. Season with salt and pepper. Cover and grill for about 10–15 minutes or until the fish reaches the desired temperature (at least 145 degrees in the thickest part).

Serve it at the table directly on the plank for a nice presentation.

Grilling Secret #1
Have a hard time cooking fish? Have no fear! The plank is here! Cooking on a plank is nearly foolproof and creates moist fish every time. Try this same recipe using cedar, cherry, or hickory wood planks.

Grilled Flatbread with Salmon, Hummus, and Fresh Herbs

Makes six 4 x 4 inch squares.

Using leftover grilled salmon from page 2, here's a yummy appetizer or easy hors d'oeuvre for another meal.

You'll need a stainless steel rectangular grill pan with holes in it for this recipe.

1 cup crumbled leftover grilled salmon

1 piece of whole grain lavash flatbread

about ½ cup or more store-bought
   hummus

fresh squeezed lemon juice (use 2–3
   lemon wedges)

6 cranks of lemon pepper plus fresh
   cracked pepper

¼ teaspoon garlic powder

2 tablespoons fresh dill, diced

1 tablespoon capers

4 tablespoons diced purple onion

1 large leaf Swiss chard, diced (or use
   parsley)

cooking spray

Place a stainless steel rectangular grill pan on the grill. Preheat the grill to medium-high with the lid closed.

Once the grill is hot, open the lid, spray the lavash bread on both sides with cooking spray and place it on the grill pan using tongs. Allow to cook for a minute or two on both sides with lid closed. When the bread becomes firm and crisp like a cracker, remove immediately and place on a cutting board or serving tray. Be careful not to overcook, as grill temperatures may vary.

Add fresh lemon juice, lemon pepper, garlic powder, and diced dill to the hummus and spread evenly over the flatbread.

Sprinkle all other ingredients over top and add a little more dill. Cut bread into squares and serve immediately. For extra brightness, squeeze more fresh lemon juice on squares just before serving. This can be served room temperature.

Grilled Salmon Salad

Makes 2–3 servings.

You can make lots of great sweet and savory salads for lunch using leftover grilled salmon like the one from page 2 or from page 8.

For the salad:

mixed baby leaf lettuces

crumbles of leftover grilled salmon, chilled

Manchego cheese, sliced thin

fresh figs (if they are not in season, try sliced pear with skins on)

fresh blueberries

raw unsalted sunflower seeds

For the dressing:

(makes enough for a large bowl for 2 people)

½ cup balsamic dressing

⅓ cup honey

2–3 teaspoons of honey mustard (I really like Maille Honey Dijon® because it doesn't have a white wine taste)

1–2 cloves of garlic, smashed and minced fine

fresh cracked pepper

Combine all ingredients for the dressing in a cup and set aside.

Put all salad ingredients in the desired amounts in a large salad bowl and pour the dressing in. Mix thoroughly with tongs or salad utensils and serve.

Salmon on Cedar Plank with Cherry Salsa

Makes about 4 servings.

I love sweet and spicy flavors paired together and this cherry salsa with a little nectarine mixed in is the bomb! This is a great recipe for parties since it can be doubled and served with tortilla chips while the fish is cooking!

1 large filet of salmon, 3 lbs or about ½ lb per serving, skin left on one side optional (I used boneless wild caught salmon)

2–3 cups sweet cherries, seeded (I used a combination of Bing and Mt. Rainier)

2–3 nectarines, skins on, diced in small pieces (optional)

4 large fresh limes, juiced

4 large garlic cloves, smashed and minced

1½ cups of sweet cherry or grape tomatoes, cut into quarters

½ jalapeño pepper, seeded and diced

2–4 tablespoons fresh cilantro, diced

For the salsa:
Combine all the ingredients in a bowl and allow to sit at least an hour or more so the flavors can mingle! (If you make it the day before, it really enhances the flavors!)

Before grilling, soak the plank by setting in a sink full of water. Place a bowl of water on top of the wood to keep it submerged. The plank should be soaked between 1–3 hours prior to cooking.

Preheat grill on high with the lid closed. Remove the plank from water and dry slightly. Spray both sides with cooking spray and place the plank on the grill with the smooth side up. Allow the wood to heat up for about 5 minutes with the grill closed before adding the fish.

Once the plank is heated, carefully spray the surface with cooking spray and place the filet on the wood, skin-side down. Season with salt and pepper. Cover and grill for about 8–10 minutes.

Open lid, and spoon on the salsa, generously coating the fish. Close the lid and cook further until the fish reaches at least 145 degrees in the thickest part of the fish.

Serve at the table directly on the plank or transfer to a platter.

Try serving this with chipotle sweet potato fries cooked on the grill (pictured here)!

Grilling Secret #2
Want to save time and money?
Cooking a larger filet once will give you leftovers you can use to top salads and make wraps for easy lunches to pack for work all week.

Grilled Chipotle Sweet Potato Fries

Makes about 4 servings.

3–4 medium to large sweet potatoes (or red yams), scrubbed clean, cut into long strips with skins on (see photo for reference)

½ cup extra virgin olive oil or grape seed oil

2–3 teaspoons chipotle powder

2 teaspoons paprika

2 teaspoons garlic powder (not garlic salt)

2 teaspoons onion powder (not with salt)

sea salt to taste

Optional: once cooked, top with fresh squeezed lime juice and crumbled Cotija cheese

In a large bowl, toss all ingredients and mix together well to coat. Use a large spoon or toss with your hands covered in latex or vinyl gloves to protect your skin from the heat of the spice. If the coating seems too dry, add a little more oil before the next step.

Divide potatoes into 2 batches and wrap each batch in heavy duty tin foil.

Place foil packets directly on the grill and cook covered over medium heat, flipping them once or twice. Cook for about 15–20 minutes. To check for doneness, carefully open a packet and stick a fork into the potatoes to see if they are soft. If not, wrap it back up and cook further until tender.

Grilled Veggies with Pesto

Makes about a cup of pesto (enough top about 10 vegetables).
For tips on using a salt slab, see page xv.

For the pesto:

1½–2 cups fresh basil leaves, chopped
  (or for a more peppery taste, use 1 cup
  basil and 1 cup fresh arugula)

½ cup walnuts or pine nuts, slightly
  browned

¼ cup Parmesan cheese, grated

2 large garlic cloves, smashed and
  minced

⅓ cup or less extra virgin olive oil

dash of fresh cracked pepper

For the vegetables:

2 medium zucchini, sliced

2–3 tomatoes, sliced

2 medium squash, sliced

Preparing the grill and preheating the slab:

If you are using a gas grill, start out on a low temperature and place the Himalayan pink salt slab directly on the grill with the lid closed. Slowly increase the temperature over about 20 minutes until it reaches about 400–500 degrees (see additional notes on page xv).

If you are using a charcoal grill, once the charcoal is hot and ready, build a pile of charcoal on one side of the grill and place the slab on the opposite side so it doesn't get direct heat while it heats up. Keep lid closed and allow the slab to heat up over the course of 20 minutes.

Preparing the pesto: If you are browning the nuts before making the pesto, heat up a little olive oil in a skillet over medium high heat. Add the nuts and stir constantly until they are browned. Remove from heat immediately and set aside to cool.

In a food processor, mix all ingredients except vegetables until the consistency becomes a thick paste. If necessary add a little bit more olive oil if it is too thick.

Preparing the vegetables: Slice zucchini and yellow squash lengthwise into ½–inch thick pieces (see photo). Slice the Roma tomatoes in half and cut the base out so there are 2 flat sides. Spray vegetables lightly with cooking oil and place on the heated salt slab. Cook vegetables on one side for about 2 minutes, or until the base of vegetables begin to sizzle. Then turn them over and add the pesto to the top. If desired, cover the grill and cook for about 2 more minutes. Once the zucchini and squash are tender, they are done.

Note: The longer the vegetables are in contact with the salt slab the saltier they become.

Grilling Secret #3

No need to add salt to foods when you use pink salt slabs. The foods naturally become infused with the delicate salt seasoning when cooked!

Grilled Flatbread with Veggies, Puttanesca Sauce, Mozzarella, and Basil

Makes 1 pizza that serves 3.

Pizza is like a cup of coffee. Everyone has a certain way they like to make it their own! Use this recipe as a base to follow and have fun creating your own special version with additional toppings, cheeses, and sauces!

You'll need a grill pan with holes for this method of cooking.

1 whole wheat lavash flatbread

3 or 4 ounces of fresh mozzarella or
    buffalo mozzarella (about 5 slices)

1¼ cup store bought Puttanesca sauce

about 10 fresh basil leaves

olive oil cooking spray

Options: crushed red pepper flakes, extra
    capers, parmesan cheese

Preheat the grill to medium-high heat.

Spray the flatbread on both sides, place on grill pan, and cook for a few minutes on both sides with the lid shut. Once it is crispy like a cracker, remove the grill pan with the flatbread immediately. Set aside and coat the flatbread with sauce, cheese, and all the toppings except for basil. Place the grill pan back on the grill, close the lid, and cook until the cheese is melted. Keep watch to ensure that the bread does not burn.

Once done, top with fresh basil leaves, remove from heat, and transfer pizza to a cutting board. Let rest for about a minute and then cut into 4-inch squares.

Note: There are some great puttanesca sauces out there and most contain capers. I love the tang the capers add to the sauce and usually add a few more sprinkled on.

Grilled Flatbread with Grilled Veggies and Goat Cheese

Makes 1 pizza that serves 3.

You'll need a grill pan with holes for this method of cooking

1 whole wheat lavash flatbread

1 yellow squash, sliced into discs about
⅛ inch thick

1 zucchini, sliced into discs about ⅛ inch
thick

2 medium tomatoes, sliced

½ purple onion, sliced into discs about ⅛
inch thick

about 4 ounces of crumbled goat cheese
(or 1 small container)

1¼ cup store bought spicy marinara or
arrabiatta sauce

about 10 fresh basil leaves, cut into
pieces

olive oil cooking spray

Options: crushed red pepper flakes, extra
capers, parmesan cheese

Preheat the grill to medium-high heat.

Spray the vegetables with a little olive oil and toss them on the grill pan. Place on the grill and stir frequently. Or if desired, simply place the larger slices directly on the grill grate for nice grill marks. Turn them once or twice and remove from heat once they are tender.

Spray the flatbread on both sides, place on grill pan, and cook for a few minutes on both sides with the lid shut. Once it is crispy like a cracker, remove the grill pan with the flatbread immediately. Set aside and coat with sauce, cheese, and all the toppings except for basil. Place the grill pan back on the grill, close the lid, and cook until the cheese is melted. Keep watch to ensure that the bread does not burn.

Once done, top with basil leaves, remove from heat, transfer pizza to a cutting board. Let rest for about a minute and then cut into 4-inch squares.

Grilled Veggies with Balsamic and Guava Dressing

Makes about 4 cups of vegetables.

Grill up a bunch of these veggies and enjoy them with anything! Use the leftovers on top of the salad on page 20.

2–3 medium zucchini, sliced into discs

2–3 medium yellow squash, sliced into discs

1 medium purple onion, or sweet onion, cut into pieces

1 large portobello mushroom cap, cut into slices (or 4–5 small cremini mushrooms, sliced)

For dressing:

3 tablespoons guava jelly or preserves

2 tablespoons shallots, minced

2 teaspoons balsamic vinegar (or, if you have it, balsamic cherry vinegar)

2 tablespoons white balsamic vinegar

3 tablespoons extra virgin olive oil

3 garlic cloves, smashed and minced

3 tablespoons water

fresh black pepper

Preheat the grill and the grill pan to medium-high heat with the lid closed.

Mix all the dressing ingredients together in a food processor or place in a bowl and whisk until blended. Taste test. Add more or less vinegar if you want more tang, then set aside. Place the vegetables in a large bowl and pour the dressing over top. Stir to coat, and add pepper if desired.

Open the grill lid, and carefully spray the grill pan at an angle so that the flames don't burn you. Add the vegetables to the pan and stir several times to ensure they don't burn. Keep lid off while cooking. Once the vegetables are tender and the onions are translucent, they can be removed from the grill. Serve immediately, or use the next day on a salad!

Summer Salad with Leftover Grilled Veggies

Makes 2–4 servings.

Use the leftover grilled vegetables with guava dressing on this salad!

Green lettuce leaves or butter lettuce
   leaves, ripped into bite-sized pieces
fresh blueberries
crumbled goat cheese
raw sunflower seeds, no salt added
   preferred
dried cranberries
grilled vegetables (from recipe on
   page 18)

Combine all ingredients in desired amounts and toss.

For dressing, use a little of the leftover guava and balsamic dressing from page 18 to top the salad and enjoy!

Flatbread Appetizer with Forelle Pear, Prosciutto, and Manchego Cheese

Makes 1 flatbread cut into six 4-inch squares.

You'll need a grill pan with holes for this method of cooking.

1 whole wheat or multi-grain lavash
    flatbread

4 Forelle pears, with skins on, sliced into
    thin pieces and cored (or any kind of
    ripe pear)

about 3–4 ounces of shaved Manchego
    cheese

about 4 ounces of prosciutto, pulled apart
    and cut into small bite-sized strips

balsamic glaze

cooking spray

Optional: microgreens or diced flat
    Parsley as a garnish

Preheat the grill to medium-high heat.

Place the grill pan on the grill and preheat to medium high heat.

Spray the flatbread on both sides, place on grill pan, and cook for a few minutes on both sides with the lid shut. Once it is crispy like a cracker, remove the grill pan with the flatbread immediately. Set aside and arrange the pears, cheese, and prosciutto evenly over top of the flatbread.

Place the grill pan back on the grill. Close the lid and cook until the cheese is melted. Keep watch to ensure that the bread does not burn.

Once done, remove from heat, transfer flatbread to a cutting board, and top with fresh microgreens or diced flat-leaf parsley, if desired. Let rest for about a minute and then cut into 4-inch squares. Place each piece on a small plates and drizzle each with a zigzag of balsamic glaze. Serve immediately.

Substitutions: If you don't want to spring for prosciutto, get a good quality Black Forest Ham from your local deli instead.

Grilling Secret #4

Look for small, firm Forelle pears summer through fall. They are a beautiful tri-colored fruit with red freckles and a robust floral flavor when ripe.

Grilled Barramundi with Wasabi Aioli

Makes 2 servings.
This recipe does not require marinating.

2 3-ounce filets of barramundi

2–3 teaspoons sweet soy* (or regular
　soy sauce)

2 tablespoons honey, maple syrup, or
　agave nectar

2 cloves fresh garlic, smashed and
　minced

fresh cracked black pepper, and sea salt
　or pink salt as desired

cooking spray (I used coconut oil cooking
　spray)

Wasabi aioli (page 190)

*Sweet soy is a thicker soy sauce that
can be found at Asian markets or in the
Asian section of the grocery store.

Before grilling: Soak the plank by setting in a sink of water. Place a bowl of water on top of the wood to keep it submerged. The wood should be soaked between 1–3 hours prior to cooking.

Mix all ingredients together and coat the salmon and set aside.

Preheat grill on high with the lid closed.

Remove the plank from water and dry slightly. Spray both sides with cooking spray and place the plank on the grill with the smooth side up. Allow the wood to heat up for about 5 minutes with the grill closed before adding the fish.

Once the plank is heated, carefully spray the surface with cooking spray and place the filet on the wood skin-side down. Spoon or brush on the sauce and reduce heat slightly to medium-high. Season with salt and pepper. Cover and grill for about 10–15 minutes or until the fish reaches the desired temperature (at least 145 degrees in the thickest part).

Once done, remove plank from grill and place on table with a heating pad underneath. Top with wasabi aioli and a bowl of sweet soy for guests to drizzle on along side the spicy aioli. Serve with stir-fried brown rice and snow peas with a hint of sweet soy mixed in.

Chapter 2

Worldly Kabobs

Pork Tenderloin Kabobs with Cumin, Thyme, and Honey Mustard

Makes about 5 kabobs (about 4 servings).

Preheat gas grill on high, or prepare a charcoal grill for direct heat grilling.

The seasoning for this works best if you marinate the meat for at least 4 hours or overnight.

1 pork tenderloin, a little over a pound

½ cup honey mustard

2 tablespoons apple cider vinegar

1 teaspoon coconut sugar or turbinado sugar

1½ tablespoon cumin, ground

1½ tablespoons fresh thyme leaves, or dried thyme

2 teaspoons olive oil

fresh ground pepper

½ teaspoon sea salt or pink salt

If you are using bamboo skewers, soak 4–6 skewers in water for at least 10 minutes prior to grilling.

Slice the pork tenderloin into medallions that are about 1 inch thick and set aside.

For the marinade, mix all other ingredients in a medium-sized bowl. Take a few tablespoons out and set aside for later.

Add the meat to the remaining marinade, and mix to coat the meat evenly. Cover the bowl and place in refrigerator for at least 4 hours or more before cooking. Overnight is even better to allow the flavors to season the meat.

Remove the pork from the marinade and discard the marinade.

Slide 2 pork medallions widthwise on the skewers (add more if skewers are long enough).

Reduce the grill temperature to medium and keep lid open.

Generously spray the grill surface with cooking spray.

Place the kabobs on the grill and cook about 3–5 minutes per side, turning once. They are done once the internal temperature reaches 145 degrees.

Remove kabobs from grill and allow to rest for 2 minutes before serving. Spoon some of reserved sauce over the top of each kabob when plating.

Grilling Secret #6

The secret to this recipe is to not overcook the pork. Have a kitchen thermometer handy while grilling and once the meat has reached an internal temperature of 145 degrees, immediately take the kabobs off the grill and set aside.

Ahi Tuna Kabob with Miso Sauce

Makes about 4–6 servings.

This recipe requires marinating the fish for at least 4 hours or overnight.

about 2 lbs of ahi tuna steaks, cut into 1 to 1½ inch cubes

½ cup miso paste

¾ cup mirin (Japanese sweet rice wine)

¼ cup water

⅔ cup coconut sugar or granulated turbinado sugar or raw sugar

¼ cup Vegenaise® or mayonnaise

1 teaspoon toasted sesame seed oil (optional)

touch of cayenne pepper

8 (12-inch) wooden skewers, soaked in water about 30 minutes prior to grilling

Options: sprinkle of sesame seeds

Preheat the gas grill on high with lid closed; or, if using charcoal grill, prepare for direct heat cooking over hot charcoal.

For the marinade: In a small saucepan, heat the miso paste, mirin, water, and coconut sugar over medium heat. Stir frequently until the sugar has dissolved. Remove from heat and whisk in the Vegenaise® or mayonnaise. Add sesame seed oil, if using, and cayenne pepper. Allow to cool to room temperature.

Place the tuna chunks in a bowl and pour the cooled marinade mixture over top. Turn tuna gently until coated with the marinade. Cover and place in the refrigerator for at least an hour (or even overnight).

Prior to grilling, remove the tuna from the refrigerator and allow to sit at room temperature for about 15 minutes.

Once the grill is hot, slide the tuna chunks onto the skewers, leaving a small space between them.

Carefully coat the grill surface with cooking spray, spraying at an angle. Add the skewers directly over heat. Turn once; each side should cook about 3–4 minutes. They will be done once their internal temperature reaches 120–125 degrees for medium rare.

Remove from grill and allow to stand about 5 minutes before serving. Sprinkle with sesame seeds and black pepper, if desired.

Grilling Secret #7

This marinade is awesome with all kinds of fish steaks, like swordfish! The sweetness of the mirin and the saltiness of the miso paste work great together.

Chicken Satay with Spicy Peanut Cilantro Dipping Sauce

Makes about 4 servings.
Marinate the chicken at least 3 hours or overnight.

For the chicken and marinade:

about 1 pound of chicken tenders

¼ cup low sodium soy sauce

1 tablespoon coconut sugar, turbinado sugar, or raw sugar

about 2 tablespoons olive oil or grapeseed oil

8 (12-inch) wooden skewers, soaked in water about 30 minutes prior to grilling

For the spicy peanut sauce:

¼ cup peanuts, roasted and unsalted

1 cup all natural peanut butter, crunchy or smooth

2 tablespoons fresh garlic

about ½ cup fresh cilantro, including stems

3 teaspoons Sriracha sauce (or other type of chili sauce)

½ cup water or more

5–6 tablespoons fresh lime juice

a dash of salt

Marinating the chicken: In a small saucepan over medium heat, add soy sauce, coconut sugar, and oil. Stir and cook until the sugar is dissolved, then remove from heat and set aside to cool.

Add the cooled marinade to a medium bowl or resealable bag. Add the chicken tenders and mix to coat thoroughly. Allow to marinate in refrigerator for up to 3 hours.

You can make the sauce in advance and store it in the refrigerator for up to 5 days, if you like. In a food processor, add the peanuts and pulse slightly until they become coarse but not fine. Then add all the other ingredients and pulse a few times until ingredients are evenly distributed. Add more water if it's too thick. The sauce should be thick enough to pour with a spoon but not too thick. Set aside.

Grilling the chicken: Preheat the gas grill to high with lid closed; or, if using charcoal grill, prepare for direct heat cooking over hot charcoal.

Prior to grilling, remove the chicken from the refrigerator and allow to sit at room temperature for about 15 minutes.

Once the grill is hot, thread the chicken tenders lengthwise onto the skewers. Two tenders will easily fit on one skewer. If they feel too heavy, add another skewer through the chicken so the kabob will be easier to hold.

Carefully coat the grill surface with cooking spray, spraying at an angle. Add the skewers directly over heat. Turn once; each side should cook about 3–4 minutes. They will be done once their internal temperature reaches 165 degrees.

Remove from grill and allow to stand about 5 minutes before serving. Serve with peanut sauce for dipping.

Grilling Secret #8
Perfect for neighborhood backyard parties—the sauce is addictive, I'm warning you now! Try making the sauce with raw almond butter too! YUM.

Grilled Scallop Appetizer with Orange Mint Pesto and Purple Yam Vermicelli

Makes about 4 servings.

1½ lbs large scallops

1 cup packed mint leaves

1 cup packed fresh cilantro, including
stems is okay

½ cup raw or roasted walnuts, unsalted;
or pine nuts

3 teaspoons orange juice concentrate,
thawed*

2 large garlic cloves, minced

⅓ cup or less of extra virgin olive oil

1½ teaspoons fresh orange zest

a dash of sea salt or pink salt

½ package (about 8 ounces) purple
yam vermicelli (look for them in Asian
markets) or any kind of rice vermicelli
pasta you enjoy

8–10 (6-inch) wooden skewers, soaked in
water about 30 minutes prior to grilling

Making the pesto: You can make the pesto in advance and store it in the refrigerator for up to 5 days if you like.

In a food processor, blend mint leaves, cilantro, nuts, orange juice concentrate, garlic, oil, and 1 teaspoon of the orange zest. The consistency should be thick. If it's too thick, add a little water and blend a little more. Set aside.

Making the vermicelli: Add a few dashes of salt to a medium saucepan of water and bring to a boil. Add the noodles and stir to separate them. If they are too long to separate, you may want to break them apart first prior to adding them to the water. Allow to cook for about 3–4 minutes. Turn the heat off and let noodles stay in the water another 2 minutes. Then drain them in a colander and rinse with water. Place in a large bowl and add a drizzle of olive oil or toasted sesame seed oil and a few dashes of salt. If desired, take kitchen scissors and cut them into 6–8 inch pieces by randomly cutting into the bowl of cooked noodles. If you want to add more flavor to the noodles, mix in a teaspoon or 2 of the pesto. Set aside.

Grilling the scallops: Preheat the gas grill to high with lid closed; or if using charcoal grill, prepare for direct heat cooking over hot charcoal.

Prior to grilling, remove the scallops from the refrigerator and allow to sit at room temperature for about 15 minutes.

Once the grill is hot, take 2 skewers and add 2 scallops to each skewer widthwise. Two scallops will easily fit on 1 skewer. If they feel too heavy, add another skewer through the scallops so the kabobs will be easier to hold.

Carefully coat the grill surface with cooking spray, spraying at an angle. Also spray the scallops slightly on both sides. Add the skewers directly on the grill. Turn once. Each side should cook about 3–4 minutes. They will be done once their internal temperature reaches 120 degrees or when flesh is opaque. Remove from the grill and set aside.

Add about a cup of the cooked vermicelli to each plate. Place the skewer on top and add about a teaspoon of pesto on top of each scallop. Top with a few sprinkles of orange zest and a crank of black pepper and serve immediately.

*If you don't have frozen orange juice concentrate on hand, substitute with the zest of 1 orange.

Skewered Thai-spiced Shrimp Appetizer with Mango

Makes about 4 servings.

This recipe works best if you marinate the shrimp for up to 4 hours or more.

For the shrimp and marinade:

1 pound raw medium/large shrimp, shells
removed, deveined if desired

1 cup lite coconut milk

4 tablespoons red curry paste

2 teaspoons fresh lemongrass (or lemongrass paste)

1 teaspoon fresh ginger

2 large cloves of garlic, minced

4 tablespoons fresh lime juice

lime zest from 1 or 2 limes

1 teaspoon kaffir lime leaves, minced
fine (skip it if you can't find them at the
Asian market)

8–10 (6-inch) wooden skewers, soaked in
water about 30 minutes prior to grilling

grape tomatoes

6–8 chunks fresh mango chunks or
pineapple chunks

about ⅓ cup of melted butter (optional)

For the marinade: Add all ingredients in a bowl (except the butter) and allow to marinate covered in the refrigerator for at least 4 hours or overnight.

Grilling the shrimp: Remove the shrimp from the refrigerator about 15 minutes before it's time to grill.

Preheat the gas grill on high with lid closed; or, if using charcoal grill, prepare for direct heat cooking over hot charcoal.

While the grill is heating up, add the shrimp, grape tomatoes, and fruit chunks to the skewers. Reduce the heat to medium if you are using a gas grill.

Carefully coat the grill surface with cooking spray, spraying at an angle. Also spray the skewers slightly on both sides. Add the skewers directly on the grill. Keep the grill lid off, as these will cook very fast. Turn once. Each side should cook about 3–4 minutes. They will be done once their internal temperature reaches 115–120 degrees or when the shrimp are opaque.

Remove skewers from the grill and set on a plate. Add a squirt more of lime if desired and drizzle melted butter overtop. Serve with lime zest.

Succulent Herb-Marinated Chicken "Speedies"

Makes about 12 speedies.

Marinate the chicken at least 3 hours or overnight.

1½ to 2 pounds chicken tenders, or skinless boneless chicken breasts sliced into strips

½ cup sherry

¼ cup extra virgin olive oil

¼ cup shallots, minced

3 large cloves of garlic, minced

1 tablespoon, fresh flat-leaf parsley, minced

2 bay leaves, crumbled

1 teaspoon dried oregano

1 teaspoon dried thyme

⅛ teaspoon red chili pepper flakes

⅛ teaspoon ground white pepper

sea salt, kosher salt, or pink salt

⅓ cup water

¼ cup purple onion, chopped

2 tablespoons red wine vinegar

2 tablespoons white balsamic vinegar

12 (12-inch) wooden skewers, soaked in water about 30 minutes prior to grilling

For the marinade: Add all ingredients in a large bowl with the chicken and allow to marinate covered in the refrigerator for at least 4 hours, preferably overnight.

Grilling the chicken: Remove the chicken from the refrigerator about 15 minutes before it's time to grill.

Preheat the gas grill on high with lid closed; or, if using charcoal grill, prepare for direct heat cooking over hot charcoal.

While the grill is heating up, add the chicken to the skewers. Reduce the heat to medium if you are using a gas grill. Carefully coat the grill surface with cooking spray, spraying at an angle.

Also spray the chicken skewers slightly on both sides. Add the skewers directly on the grill. Keep the grill lid off, as these will cook very fast. Turn once; each side should cook about 5 minutes. They will be done once their internal temperature reaches 165 degrees. Remove from the grill and set on a plate.

Options: Serve with grilled fresh tomatoes. Simply cut tomatoes in half, add a little olive oil, and grill them for a few minutes on one side. Add sea salt or pink salt and fresh black pepper to taste.

Grilling Secret #9
The secret to making the Speedies is to marinate them overnight. Another easy recipe for a backyard gathering!

Persian-Style Beef Kabobs

Makes about 4 kabobs.

Marinate the beef overnight for best results.

1½ pounds beef tips (I used Black
    Angus), cut into 1-inch cubes

1½ cup extra virgin olive oil

2 teaspoons sumac

1 teaspoon cinnamon

8 cranks of pink salt (about 2 teaspoons)

6 cranks of fresh ground pepper

1 tablespoon honey

2 tablespoons apricot preserves

zest of 1 lemon

2 teaspoons lemon juice

½ teaspoon garlic powder

1 teaspoon ginger paste or fresh ginger,
    grated

⅓ cup water

4 (12-inch) wooden skewers, soaked in
    water about 30 minutes prior to grilling

fresh mint for garnish

For the marinade: Add all ingredients together (except beef and mint leaves) and stir to mix. Then remove about ¼ cup of sauce and set aside for pouring over the kabobs when serving.

Add the beef to the large bowl of marinade. Stir to coat the meat thoroughly. Cover bowl with plastic wrap and allow to marinate covered in the refrigerator for at least 4 hours, preferably overnight.

Grilling the beef: Remove the beef from the refrigerator about 15 minutes before it's time to grill and discard the marinade.

Preheat the gas grill on high with lid closed; or, if using charcoal grill, prepare for direct heat cooking over hot charcoal.

While the grill is heating up, add the beef to the skewers. Reduce the heat to medium if you are using a gas grill. Carefully coat the grill surface with cooking spray, spraying at an angle. Also lightly spray the skewers on both sides and place skewers directly on the grill. Keep the grill lid off, as these will cook very fast. Turn once; each side should cook about 5–7 minutes or until the internal temperature reaches 145 degrees. Remove from the grill and set on a plate. Spoon the extra marinade that had been set aside over top of the kabobs, garnish with mint, and serve immediately.

Options: Serve with grilled vegetable kabobs made with whole grape tomatoes and slices of purple onion, or sweet white onion. Spray a little cooking oil on each kabob, add a little fresh black pepper and sea salt or pink salt, and grill until they are tender, or until the onions are slightly transparent.

Tangy Grilled Tofu Teriyaki Kabobs with Veggies and Pineapple

Makes about 12 6-inch kabobs.
Marinating the tofu makes this much tastier—trust me, you'll want to do this overnight.

1 12-ounce package extra firm tofu, cut into 1-inch cubes and patted dry with a paper towel

about 1½ cups store-bought teriyaki sauce (I use SoyVay® Veri Veri Teriyaki Sauce®)

fresh black pepper or coarsely ground black pepper

1 sweet bell pepper, any color, seeded and cut into slices

1 medium zucchini, sliced into ½ inch thick pieces

about 6–8 cubes of fresh pineapple

6–8 cherry tomatoes or grape tomatoes

about 6–8 pieces of purple onion or sweet white onion

sesame seeds to garnish (optional)

12 (12-inch) wooden skewers, soaked in water about 30 minutes prior to grilling

For the marinade: In a medium sized bowl, add the tofu chunks and about ½ cup of the teriyaki sauce. Add a few shakes of black pepper. Carefully stir to coat the tofu chunks with sauce.

Place the vegetables and pineapple chunks in another medium sized bowl. Mix the remaining teriyaki sauce and black pepper and set aside about ¼ cup (to pour over kabobs when serving) before adding sauce to vegetables and fruit; stir to coat.

Cover both bowls with plastic wrap and place in the refrigerator overnight.

Cooking the kabobs: Preheat the gas grill on high with lid closed; or, if using charcoal grill, prepare for direct heat cooking over hot charcoal.

While the grill is heating up, add the tofu, pineapple, and vegetables to the skewers.

Reduce the heat to medium if you are using a gas grill.

Carefully coat the grill surface with cooking spray, spraying at an angle. Lighty spray the kabobs on both sides with cooking spray and place them directly on the grill.

Keep the grill lid off and cook and cook for about 5 minutes on each side. Carefully turn once while cooking.

Remove from the grill and set on a plate. Spoon the extra sauce that had been set aside over the top of the kabobs and serve immediately. Top with toasted sesame seeds, if desired.

Grilling Secret #10

Let's face it—tofu on its own is just not very sexy, am I right? Tofu is so healthy yet it's really flavorless unless you marinate it. Be sure to use extra firm tofu so the cubes don't fall apart on the grill. Use tongs or a spatula to flip the kabobs.

Greek Chicken and Veggie Kabob

Makes about 4 servings.

This recipe works best when the chicken is marinated overnight.

For the chicken marinade:

3 chicken breasts, skinless, boneless, sliced diagonally into about 1-inch strips

1 cup non-fat plain Greek-style yogurt

⅓ cup fresh lemon juice plus 2 tablespoons

5 cranks of fresh black pepper (about 2 teaspoons)

4 cranks fresh ground sea salt or pink salt, (1 teaspoon each)

3 tablespoons fresh mint leaves, chopped

5 large garlic cloves, smashed and minced fine (about 2 tablespoons)

1 tablespoon honey

1–2 yellow squash

10–14 cherry or grape tomatoes

1–2 medium-sized zucchini

slices of purple onion, cut wide (optional)

1 package frozen, fully cooked brown rice

drizzle of olive oil

squirt of lemon juice

sea or pink salt and fresh ground pepper, to taste

1 teaspoon minced mint leaves

5–6 (12-inch) wooden skewers, soaked in water about 30 minutes prior to grilling

Making the marinade: In a large bowl add all the ingredients except the chicken and vegetables and stir. Once mixed together, add the chicken. Cover bowl with plastic wrap or transfer all ingredients to a recloseable bag and place in refrigerator overnight.

Grilling the chicken: Preheat the gas grill on high with lid closed; or, if using charcoal grill, prepare for direct heat cooking over hot charcoal.

Prior to grilling, remove the chicken from the refrigerator and allow to sit at room temperature for about 15 minutes.

Once the grill is hot, loosely thread about 4–5 chunks of chicken on each skewer and set aside. Carefully coat the grill surface with cooking spray, spraying at an angle. Add the skewers directly over heat. Turn once. Each side should cook about 3–5 minutes. They will be done once their internal temperature reaches 165 degrees.

Grilling the vegetables: Thread the vegetables on skewers and spray with a little cooking oil. Add the skewers directly over heat. Turn once. Each side should cook about 2–3 minutes or until tender.

Preparing brown rice: Heat up brown rice according to package instructions. Place in a bowl with a drizzle of olive oil, a squirt of lemon, sea salt or pink salt, and fresh ground black pepper. Add about a teaspoon of minced mint leaves and stir.

To serve, once the kabobs are cooked either arrange them over top of a platter of the rice and serve family style, or remove the skewers from the kabobs and toss the chicken and vegetables in with the rice and plate individually. Serve with a fresh lemon wedge.

BBQ Meatball Kabobs

Makes about 12–14 2-inch meatballs.

2 pounds ground beef or ground turkey

1 large sweet white onion, finely minced

¾ cup whole wheat flour

4 tablespoons store-bought hickory
  barbeque sauce

1 teaspoon grape seed oil or olive oil

⅓ cup Parmesan cheese, grated (or use
  half Parmesan and half grated Asiago
  cheese)

3 large garlic cloves, minced

2 tablespoons dried parsley or fresh flat-
  leaf parsley, sliced

½ teaspoon pink salt, or sea salt

½ teaspoon fresh ground black pepper
  (about 4–5 cranks)

2 eggs, whisked

4–5 metal skewers

add a few dashes of cayenne pepper for
  added kick, if desired

Preparing the meatballs: In a large bowl mix all the ingredients except the meat. Using your hands, add in the ground beef or turkey and blend the ingredients until mixed thoroughly. Form into meatballs about 1½ to 2 inches in diameter, and set aside on a plate. Continue to do this until meatballs are all formed.

Preheat the gas grill on high with lid closed; or, if using charcoal grill, prepare for direct heat cooking over hot charcoal.

Once the grill is hot, loosely thread about 4–5 meatballs on each skewer, and set aside.

Skewer 1 meatball at a time alternating with pieces of onion and bell pepper. Place kebobs on a lightly oiled grill grate and allow to cook for 10 minutes, rotating every 2–3 minutes. Remove from heat and serve.

Grilling Secret #11
If you want to add another layer of flavor, add some applewood or hickory chips to your grill and these meatballs will be even better! Make extra—the kids will love them!

Simple Summer Chicken and Veggie Kabob with Italian Dressing Marinade

Makes about 4 servings.

You don't need to marinate this overnight, but it does taste great if you can allow it to marinate for at least 2 hours prior to grilling.

1¾ cups good quality all natural Italian dressing (I really like Newman's Own Tuscan Italian Organic Dressing®)

1 pound chicken breasts, boneless, skinless, cut into 1-inch cubes

1 red, yellow, or orange bell pepper

1 sweet onion, cut in thick strips

1 medium zucchini, cut into ½-inch discs

1–2 yellow squash, ½-inch discs

6–8 cremini mushrooms

fresh black pepper

8–10 (12-inch) wooden skewers, soaked in water about 30 minutes prior to grilling

For the salad: fresh basil leaves, sliced (optional)
4–6 cups baby leaf lettuces or butter lettuce leaves

For the marinade: In a large bowl, add all the ingredients including chicken (reserving ¼ cup of dressing for salad) and stir to coat. Cover bowl with plastic wrap and place in refrigerator for at least an hour or longer before grilling.

Grilling the chicken: Preheat the gas grill on high with lid closed; or if using charcoal grill, prepare for direct heat cooking over hot charcoal.

Prior to grilling, remove the chicken from the refrigerator and allow to sit at room temperature for about 15 minutes.

Once the grill is hot, loosely thread chunks of chicken and vegetables on each skewer, and set aside.

Carefully coat the grill surface with cooking spray, spraying at an angle. Add the skewers directly over heat. Turn once. Each side should cook about 3–5 minutes. They will be done once their internal temperature reaches 165 degrees.

To serve, in a large bowl, toss remaining ¼ cup dressing with the greens. Remove the chicken and vegetables from the skewers and toss on top of the greens. Sprinkle with fresh basil and fresh cracked pepper. Serve immediately.

Chapter 3

Stuff It. Wrap It. Tie it up!

Stuffed Butternut Squash with Sweet Sausage and Farro

Makes 2 large slices (about 4 servings).

1 large butternut squash

1 cup farro

1 ½ cups water

extra virgin olive oil

1 crank of salt (about ½ a teaspoon)

2–4 sweet sausage (I used chicken apple sausage),

1 apple (any kind of sweet apple)

fresh thyme

Cooking the farro: Combine farro, water, a drizzle of oil, and salt in a medium sauce pan and bring to a boil. Reduce to simmer, and cover. Cook for another 25–30 minutes or until the farro is tender yet chewy.

Grilling the squash (you can grill the sausage at the same time): Preheat gas grill on high with lid closed; or, if using charcoal grill, prepare for direct heat cooking over hot charcoal. If you are using a gas grill, reduce the temperature of the grill to medium-high. Carefully coat the grill surface with cooking spray, spraying at an angle.

Slice the squash lengthwise and remove seeds and stringy bits. Coat with olive oil or cooking spray and place skin side down on the grill with the lid open. Grill for about 15–20 minutes, then flip pieces over for another 10 minutes or until it is fork tender. Then remove from grill and set aside for filling.

Grilling the chicken apple sausage and apple: Slice sausage lengthwise if you wish to have nice grill marks for extra pieces. If not, leave them whole. Grill the chicken sausage until the internal temperature reaches 165 degrees then remove from heat. Slice and core apple wedges, coat with a little olive oil or cooking spray, and add them to the outer edges of the grill for about 1 minute on each side. You can leave skins on if desired.

Preparing the farro stuffing: In a medium bowl, add the farro and 1 length of the sausage diced fine. Add in some diced apple, a little salt, and some fresh thyme. Mix together with a spoon and fill the hole in each side of the butternut squash.

Serve with the remaining apple and chicken apple sausage.

Grilling Secret #12

You can also cook the sliced butternut squash wrapped in tin foil directly on the grill. It will cook a bit faster. In the fall, look for small sugar pumpkins and try those for this recipe. They are super sweet.

Stuffed Rainbow Trout

Serves about 4—plus a cat or 2 if you don't watch the picnic table!

You'll need some cotton string for this. Make sure to use an all-natural string or twine that is not synthetic for tying up your fish. You can cook this immediately or allow to marinate for about 30 minutes or more if you wish.

1 large rainbow trout, whole, gutted

extra-virgin olive oil for drizzling

2–3 lemons, sliced thin

fresh tomato slices

a few thin slices of sweet Vidalia onion

plenty of fresh black pepper and sea salt
   or pink salt

1 tablespoon garlic, chopped (about 3
   large cloves)

8 fresh oregano sprigs

about 2 teaspoons capers

green olives, pitted and diced

butter

Options: Grill some grape tomatoes alongside the fish on some skewers.

Preparing the grill: Prepare a charcoal or gas grill for direct grilling over medium-high heat with the lid closed.

Preparing the fish: Have your fishmonger slice and gut the fish. He may or may not debone it for you. For nicer presentation, ask him to leave the fins and head on, if desired.

Lay the fish in a 9 x 12-inch casserole dish or a flat tray and drizzle olive oil on the inside of the fish. Add thin slices of lemon and cover the length of the fish. Add thin slices of tomato and onion. Add a few cranks of fresh black pepper, salt, garlic, and oregano leaves. Sprinkle capers and the diced olives. Top with a few pats of butter. Fold the fish closed.

Cut 8 strands of string, each about 12 inches in length. Begin tying up the fish carefully so that it's not too tight but still keeps the stuffing inside. Continue tying the fish about every 2–3 inches along the length of the fish.

Once the grill is hot, carefully spray both sides of the fish with cooking spray. Spray the grill directly at an angle as well. Using 2 spatulas, carefully place the fish directly on the grill. Cover the grill and reduce temperature down to medium-high (if using a gas grill). Turn the fish once and cook about 5–6 minutes per side. Fish is done when it reaches an internal temperature of 145 degrees in the thickest part of the fish. Serve immediately on a large platter with a bed of baby greens and grilled grape tomatoes, if desired. Serve with lemon wedges.

Grilling Secret # 13

For an extra level of sweet smoky flavor, use about 2 cups of applewood chunks and soak them in water for about 30 minutes. Place them at the bottom of the grill in a wood smoker box, if you have one, or simply wrap them in tin foil; poke several holes in the foil and place the bundle at the bottom of the grill next to the charcoal.

Stuffed Yam with Garbanzo Beans, Quinoa, and Fennel

Makes 2 halves (2–4 servings).

1 large yam (or sweet potato)

1 cup cooked quinoa (look for the fully cooked kind in the grocery aisle!)

½ cup fennel bulb (and some of the fronds)

¼ cup canned garbanzo beans (chick peas), rinsed and drained

2 tablespoons fresh basil leaves, julienne cut (with a little extra for topping)

2½ teaspoons rice vinegar (seasoned or unseasoned is fine)

2 teaspoons olive oil

1 teaspoon honey or blue agave nectar

Grilling the yam: Scrub and wash the yam, leaving the skin on. For faster cook time, slice the yam in half lengthwise. Drizzle a little olive oil or cooking spray on the cut sides and cover each piece in tin foil.

Preheat gas grill on high with lid closed; or, if using charcoal grill, prepare for direct heat cooking over hot charcoal. Place the yams directly on the grill for about 10–15 minutes turning once. To check for doneness, move the yam over to the edge of the grill, open the foil, and stick a knife through to see if it's tender. If it's not, seal up and place back in the center of the grill until tender.

Once done, remove the yams from the grill and allow to cool about 10 minutes. Remove the foil.

Preparing the stuffing: While the yam is cooling slightly, add the remaining ingredients to a medium-sized bowl and mix through. Once the yam is cool enough to handle, take a knife and cut crisscross slices on the open-faced side of the yam, then remove some of the chunks. Be careful not to cut into the bottom part of the skin. If desired, scoop out more of the yam with a spoon, add it to the bowl, and mix with the other ingredients. Then carefully stuff the yam with the mixture. Top with a little extra sliced basil and/or fennel fronds and serve immediately.

Options: Serve with fresh grilled corn and homemade lime and mint sparking water! YUM! If you like, add a tiny bit of blue agave nectar if you want it sweet—it's super refreshing.

Grilled Stuffed Banana Peppers with Goat Cheese, Pine Nuts, and Golden Raisins

Makes 8 slices.

This is a yummy little appetizer or can even be made as a side dish. The trick is, store-bought banana peppers are sometimes mild and sometimes hot. You may not know which kind you get unless you grow your own! Both kinds will work with this recipe!

8 banana peppers

2 medium apples, diced into small pieces

about ½ cup of crumbled goat cheese
   (plain, not herbed)

about ¼ cup of pine nuts (or chopped
   walnuts), chopped

Preheat gas grill on medium with lid closed; or, if using charcoal grill, prepare for direct heat cooking over medium heat charcoal or indirect heat.

Slice a sliver off each pepper lengthwise to create an open "boat." Remove the seeds and discard core.

In a medium bowl combine all other ingredients to make the filling mixture.

Stuff the peppers and pack it with a spoon or your fingers.

Once the grill is ready, spray the bottom of each pepper with a little cooking spray and place on the grill using tongs or a spatula. If desired, use a grill grate so they don't fall through the cracks of the grill. Close the lid and cook for about 10 minutes. Once they are slightly charred on the bottom, place them on tin foil and continue cooking until the filling on top begins to brown.

Serve immediately.

Grilling Secret #14:
Use disposable latex or vinyl gloves to work with the peppers in case they turn out to be hot peppers. No matter how much you wash your hands, hot pepper juice is hard to get off. Be sure to rinse your cutting board right away.

Salmon Parcel Cooked in Cedar Paper with Dill and Horseradish Sauce

Makes 8–10 parcels.

Parcels make a fun little appetizer for a party! The cedar paper can be found in barbeque stores or sometimes in summer seasons at the grocery store near the charcoal display.

Salmon filet, skinless, boneless

For the cedar parcels:

fresh dill

4–5 lemon wedges

3 large garlic cloves, smashed and
   minced fine

Dijon mustard (about ½ teaspoon per
   parcel)

a little sea salt or pink salt

1 package of 8 cedar paper wrappers (6 x 8
   inch is what I used and I cut them in half)

8–10 (4–6 inch) bamboo skewers that
   have been soaked in water for about
   30 minutes

cherry or grape tomatoes to serve on the
   side (optional)

For the sauce:

¼ cup prepared horseradish

about 2 teaspoons fresh lemon juice
   (or more)

⅓ cup Vegenaise® or mayonnaise, or
   plain non-fat Greek-style yogurt

1 scallion, minced fine

black pepper

4 tablespoons (give or take) fresh dill,
   minced

To prep the cedar paper: Place a few inches of water in a shallow dish or sink and soak the cedar paper for 30 minutes prior to grilling. Soak the bamboo skewers at the same time.

To make the sauce: In a small bowl mix all ingredients and set aside.

To prep the grill: Preheat gas grill on medium with lid closed; or, if using charcoal grill, prepare for direct heat cooking over medium-high heat charcoal.

To fill and wrap the parcels: Slice the salmon filets into 2 x 3-inch pieces. Place 1 piece in the center of the wrapper that's been cut to 3 x 8 inches in size, approximately. Add a sprig of fresh dill, a dollop of Dijon mustard and a thin wedge of lemon. Sprinkle with a few chunks of garlic in each wrapper. Top with a dash of salt and fresh cracked pepper. Roll up each side of paper and fold over the sides. Skewer the package through the fish to seal the paper together. Prepare the remaining parcels.

To grill the parcels: At an angle, carefully spray the grill grate with some cooking oil. Place the parcels directly on the grill. Cover and allow to cook for about 3–4 minutes per side or until the internal temperature of the fish reaches 145 degrees.

Serve with grilled skewered grape tomatoes, if desired, and the sauce.

Grilling Secrets #15

Look for cedar wrapper packs in the grilling aisle during summer. Off season, look for them online. Fire and Flavor makes them and they are available at Amazon.com for about $7.00 for a pack of 6. Wildwood Grilling has a store on Etsy.com and makes both cedar and alder wood wraps.

Portobello Mushroom Appetizer topped 3 ways

Makes about 1 cup.

Portobello mushroom caps are so versatile to use as an appetizer because you can top them with virtually anything you have left over in the fridge. Here (on this page and the following spread) are 3 ways you can top them for your next dinner party—along with a simple basil pesto to dress it up.

Quick basil pesto:

1 cup fresh basil leaves, roughly chopped

½ cup arugula* (or if you don't have it, just use more basil)

3 tablespoons extra virgin olive oil

2 large garlic cloves

2 tablespoons pine nuts, or raw walnuts

2 tablespoons water

4–5 cranks of salt (or about ½ teaspoon)

2 cranks of fresh cracked pepper (or about 2 teaspoons)

In a food processor, mix all ingredients together and set aside.

*Arugula adds a nice peppery taste to the sauce.

Portobello Mushrooms Topped with Farro, Sundried Tomatoes, and Basil Pesto

2 portobello mushroom caps

½ cup farro (yields 1 cup cooked)

1½ cups water or vegetable broth

4–5 tablespoons chopped sundried tomatoes (the kind that comes in a jar with olive oil, or find them on a salad bar)

4 tablespoons basil pesto sauce

Combine farro, water or broth, a drizzle of oil, and salt in a medium saucepan and bring to a boil. Reduce to simmer, and cover. Cook for another 25–30 minutes or until the farro is tender yet chewy. Once done, stir in the sundried tomatoes and set aside.

Preheat gas grill on medium with lid closed; or, if using charcoal grill, prepare for direct heat cooking over medium heat charcoal or indirect heat.

Drizzle or spray each mushroom cap with a little olive oil cooking spray and place directly on the grill. Cook for about 3–4 minutes per side, turning once. Transfer to a serving plate with the gill side facing up. Generously fill with the farro mixture. Top with a dollop of basil pesto and serve immediately.

Options: Place back on the grill for about 2–3 minutes and top with shaved parmesan cheese.

Portobello Mushrooms topped with Purple Kale, Goat Cheese, and Grilled Apple

2 portobello mushroom caps

2 cups purple kale, destemmed, chopped fine (or use any kind of kale)

½ cup crumbled goat cheese

¾ cup dried cranberries, chopped

1 medium-sized apple, cut into ⅛ discs for grilling (I used Pink Lady apples)

minced flat-leaf parsley or cilantro to garnish (optional)

Preheat gas grill on medium with lid closed; or, if using charcoal grill, prepare for direct heat cooking over medium heat charcoal or indirect heat.

Add chopped kale to a medium-sized bowl and drizzle with a little olive oil. Gently massage the kale with fingers to distribute the olive oil and soften the leaves. Add goat cheese and dried cranberries and set aside.

Drizzle or spray each mushroom cap with a little olive oil cooking spray and place directly on the grill. Cook for about 3–4 minutes per side, turning once. When done, remove and place on serving plate gill side up.

Grill the slices of apple on the outer edges of the grill for about 1 minute and remove to cool. Once cooled, core the center, dice into small pieces, and add to the kale mixture.

Generously fill the mushroom cap with the topping and serve.

Portobello Mushroom Topped Grilled Chicken Apple Sausage and Arugula

2 portobello mushroom caps

2 chicken apple sausage links (or any kind of sweet Italian sausage)

1 cup fresh arugula, chopped

½ cup walnuts

fresh cracked pepper

drizzle of extra virgin olive oil

sea salt or pink salt to taste

Preheat gas grill on medium with lid closed; or, if using charcoal grill, prepare for direct heat cooking over medium heat charcoal or indirect heat.

Cook the sausage and mushroom caps at the same time. Drizzle or spray each mushroom cap with a little olive oil cooking spray and place directly on the grill. Cook for about 3–4 minutes per side, turning once, then set aside on serving plate gill side up. Next, place whole sausage links directly on the grill and spray lightly with cooking oil. Once done, remove from heat and allow to cool enough to handle. Cut into small strips or dice fine.

In a medium-sized bowl, mix arugula, walnuts, diced sausage, and a drizzle of olive oil. Add salt and pepper to taste.

Generously fill the mushroom cap with the topping and serve.

Grilled Mahi Mahi Tacos topped with Mango Salsa and Chipotle Sweet Potato Fries

Makes about 4 servings (2 tacos each).

This recipe is terrific any time of year, but such a great "go to" dish for any simple neighborhood gathering. If mangoes are not in season, don't bother making the salsa—the frozen spears just don't have any flavor for the salsa. (Grilling secret bonus tip: Make the salsa a day in advance for even more spectacular flavor!) See page 10 for Chipotle Yam Fries recipe. You can use sweet potatoes or yams.

For the fish:

2 4-ounce (give or take) mahi mahi filets

1 squeeze of lime juice

1 dash red pepper flakes

1 pinch of sea salt

drizzle of olive oil

handful of fresh, diced garlic

white corn or flour tortillas

For the mango salsa:

1½ cups of tomatoes (I prefer grape tomatoes, unless fresh summer tomatoes are available)

1 tablespoon jalapeño pepper, stemmed, seeded, and minced

4–6 large cloves of garlic, smashed and minced

½ of a purple onion, diced

¼ cup fresh cilantro leaves, chopped (more or less to taste)

3–4 limes, juiced, plus extra wedges to serve

1–2 ripe, large ripe mangoes cut into small cubes (or 3–4 Ataúlfo mangoes, also called Champagne mangoes)

dash of sea salt or pink salt

To prep the fish: Toss all the fish ingredients with the mahi mahi in a plastic bag and marinate for at least 30 minutes or more in the refrigerator. Bring it out of the refrigerator about 15 minutes prior to grilling.

To make the mango salsa: Combine all the mango salsa ingredients in a medium-sized bowl and set aside.

Options: Serve with slivered purple or white cabbage, grilled halves of tomatillos, and grilled ears of corn. Serve with diced avocado.

Preheat gas grill on medium with lid closed; or, if using charcoal grill, prepare for direct heat cooking over medium-high heat charcoal.

Carefully spray the grill grate with cooking spray or lightly brush on cooking oil. Add the filets to the grill and allow to cook with lid closed for about 5 minutes per side. The fish will be done when it reaches 145 degrees and becomes flakey. Remove immediately. If desired, grill the tortilla wraps for about 30 seconds per side to heat through and remove.

Flake fish into bite-sized pieces. Add a few pieces of fish to each tortilla. Add shredded cabbage and mango salsa. Squeeze fresh lime juice on top of filling and serve immediately.

Grilling Secret #16
Can't find fresh mahi mahi? Try tilapia, grouper, or ono instead.

Stuffed Grilled Yam with Cashew Crema

Makes 2 halves (2–4 servings).

1 large yam (or large sweet potato)

1 cup quinoa, fully cooked (look for this in the freezer case or grocery aisle)

½ bunch rainbow chard, chopped (about 2 cups)

2 tomatillos, cut in half, with the outer husk removed

1 ear of corn, in the husk

¾ cup canned black beans, drained and rinsed

2 cranks of fresh cracked salt (about ½ teaspoon)

2 cranks of fresh black pepper (about ½ teaspoon)

½ teaspoon sumac

¼ cup fresh cilantro leaves

1 batch Cashew Crema (page 76)

tin foil

Grilling Secret #17

Want to impress your vegan friends? Serve this vegan recipe. You can also make the Cashew Crema without the chipotle powder and drizzle it on top of fresh fruit or a vegan brownie for dessert.

Grill the yam, corn, and tomatillo at the same time.

For the yam: Scrub and wash the yam, leaving the skin on. For faster cook time, slice the yam in half lengthwise. Drizzle a little olive oil or cooking spray on the cut sides and cover each piece in tin foil.

Preheat gas grill on high with lid closed; or, if using charcoal grill, prepare for direct heat cooking over hot charcoal. Place the yams directly on the grill for about 10–15 minutes, turning once. To check for doneness, move the yam over to the edge of the grill, open the foil and stick a knife through to see if it's tender. If it's not, seal up and place back to the center of the grill until tender. Once done, remove the potatoes from the grill and allow to cool about 10 minutes. Remove the foil. Once cooled enough to handle, take a knife and make criscross cuts into open-faced side to cube. Remove some of the yam or potato cubes and place in a large bowl.

For the corn cob: Pull the husk down about ½ way and remove as much of the silk as possible. Rinse the corn with cold water and fold the husk back in place to cover the corn. Place directly on the grill and cook for about 15 minutes, turning every 5 minutes. Set aside to cool. Once cooled, take a knife and cut kernels off the cob and place in the bowl with the yam or potato.

For the tomatillos: Remove the outer husks and rinse the tomatillos. Slice in half. Spray with a little cooking oil and place directly on the grill grate for about 2 minutes per side until charred. Remove to cool. Dice into small pieces and place in the bowl with corn and yam or potato.

Assembly: In a small sauce pan or microwave, heat up the fully cooked quinoa and beans. Then add to the bowl with corn, tomatillos, and potato. Place all the remaining ingredients in the bowl and mix gently. Taste test and add more salt or sumac to taste. Take the mixture and place it back into the 2 potato skins. Add a few fresh cilantro leaves to top, and drizzle cashew crema (page 76) over top. Serve immediately.

Cashew Crema

Makes 1 cup.

You'll need to make this overnight. For a killer salad dressing, double this recipe and top off your favorite greens! The crema will store in the refrigerator for 4–5 days.

1 cup raw unsalted cashews

¾ cup water

1½ teaspoon lemon juice

½ teaspoon smoked salt (if you have it)
   or use 1 teaspoon pink salt or sea salt

1 teaspoon chipotle powder

Place cashews in a bowl and cover them with cold water. Cover and refrigerate overnight.

Drain the cashews and rinse under cold water.

Place the cashews in a food processor and add about ½ cup cold water. Blend on high until the mixture is very smooth. If necessary add about another ⅓ cup of water and blend further. Add lemon juice, smoked salt, and chipotle powder and blend for another few seconds. The consistency should be like a thick salad dressing that you could pour.

Campfire Burgers

Makes 8 burgers.

For this recipe, it's most fun using a hardwood charcoal grill instead of a gas grill.

For the burgers:

2 pounds ground beef or ground turkey

2 tablespoons Worcestershire sauce

½ teaspoon garlic powder

½ teaspoon onion powder or onion
    granules

2 capfuls of liquid smoke (optional)

2 medium bay leaves, crushed up

1 egg, whisked

¾ cup ketchup

4 tablespoons mustard

plenty of fresh cracked pepper and sea
    salt or pink salt

2–3 sweet peppers, seeded and sliced
    into strips (I used red and yellow)

1–2 purple or sweet onion, sliced into
    wedges

Other options: sliced zucchini, yellow
    squash, and sliced mushrooms

heavy-duty tin foil

Mix all the burger ingredients in a large bowl. Take 2 pieces of heavy duty tin foil and set them on the counter. Spray the center with a little cooking spray. Form a ball of burger meat and place it in the middle of the tin foil. Add in slices of sweet peppers and onions to each and fold up the sides to seal the packages completely. Continue forming the campfire burger packages until ingredients are all used up. If you are camping in a group and some folks have added other ingredients to make it their own, take a marker and add their names to the tin foil so you know whose is whose.

Remove the grill grate from the grill. Fill a charcoal chimney with hardwood charcoal and place at the base of the grill. Place some crumpled newspaper underneath the chimney and light carefully with a match. After the coals have heated up and are red at the top of the chimney, carefully flip the chimney over and dump the coals into the base of the grill. Spread them out evenly on the bottom of the grill. Allow them to cool for about 5 minutes prior to adding the parcels.

Place the burger parcels directly on the coals and cook for about 10–12 minutes turning every 5 minutes. Coal temperatures will vary greatly, so after about 10 minutes remove one of the parcels and open up the tin foil to check to see if it's done.

When the internal temperature of the burger reaches about 160 degrees, remove the parcels and serve in tin foil. Add additional condiments if desired.

Grilled Acorn Squash Stuffed with Farro, Fresh Fig, and Goat Cheese

Makes about 4–5 center-cut pieces.

1 acorn squash, sliced into discs
   (method below)

5 or 6 fresh figs, sliced in half

2 tablespoons crumbled goat cheese

1 tablespoon fresh basil leaves, thinly
   sliced

1 tablespoon pecans, preferably
   unsalted, chopped

1 tablespoon dried cranberries, chopped

1 crank of coarse salt (about ½
   teaspoon)

1 crank of fresh cracked pepper

olive oil

cooking spray

For the farro:

1 cup farro

2 cups water or vegetable broth

1 tablespoon fresh oregano, chopped
   (dried is okay too)

2 cranks of coarse salt

1 crank pepper

¼ teaspoon blue agave nectar, honey, or
   maple syrup

Combine farro, water or broth, oregano, and salt and pepper in a medium saucepan. Bring to a boil over high heat. Reduce to simmer, and cover. Cook for another 25–30 minutes or until the farro is tender yet chewy. Add the blue agave nectar or honey at the end and remove from heat. Transfer to a large bowl.

While the farro is cooking, preheat gas grill on high with lid closed; or, if using charcoal grill, prepare for direct heat cooking over hot charcoal.

Rinse and scrub the acorn squash. While holding the squash with one hand, place it on the cutting board and carefully cut into the squash with the tip of a sharp knife. Rock it into the squash to cut it into 4 5½-inch rings depending on the size of squash. Remove the seeds and fibers from the center of the squash. Brush with olive oil or spray cooking spray on each side and set aside. Place squash directly on the grill for about 3 minutes per side or until they are tender. Remove from grill and place directly on serving dish.

Slice figs in half lengthwise and brush or spray with olive oil. Place on grill grate with tongs and cook for just 45 seconds to a minute to get grill marks, and remove immediately.

Once the figs are cool enough to handle, take 5–6 of the slices, cut into small pieces, and add into the bowl of farro. Add in goat cheese, diced cranberries, some of the basil, and pecans. Stir gently. Add salt and pepper to taste. With a spoon, fill the acorn rings and tamp down with the back of the spoon. Top with a few more bits of chopped basil and serve.

Grilling Secret #18

Looks like too many steps? Make these ahead of time for your party. Once cooked, place in the fridge for up to 3 days. Then on the day of the party, simply place some tin foil on the grill, transfer the acorn squash to the grill with a metal spatula, and reheat.

Grilled Ham Quesadilla with Manchego Cheese and Fig

about 2 ounces Black Forest ham per
quesadilla

large tortilla wraps

a few fresh figs, sliced into discs

fresh baby lettuces (or any kind of
greens)

grated Manchego cheese

cooking spray

options serve with fresh fruit and berries

Preheat gas grill on high with lid closed; or, if using char-coal grill, prepare for direct heat cooking over hot charcoal.

Add grated cheese on top of a whole quesadilla. Then top with ham, greens, and some sliced figs. Top again with a little more cheese and a second tortilla.

Once grill is hot, spray grill grate with a little cooking oil and carefully transfer the quesadillas onto the grill using metal spatulas. Cook for about 2 minutes on each side; or until the cheese has melted and the grill marks are visible on the quesadilla.

Remove and allow to cool slightly before cutting in half. Serve immediately.

Grilling Secret #19

Elevate your next tailgate party and bring these yummy quesadillas! Assemble ahead of time and stack them in a plastic container—just pop them in the cooler until you are ready to grill. For another variety, use smoked turkey.

Grilled Stuffed Spaghetti Squash topped with Puttanesca Sauce

Makes 2 halves—so good you may want to double this recipe!

1 large spaghetti squash

1–1½ cups store-bought Puttanesca or Arrabiatta sauce

fresh basil and/or parsley, chopped

2 tablespoons Kalamata olives, pitted and sliced

1 tablespoon capers

about ⅓ cup Manchego cheese, shaved

a few shakes of red chili pepper flakes

olive oil cooking spray or regular cooking spray

2 pieces of heavy duty tin foil

Grilling the squash: (you can grill the sausage at the same time):

Preheat gas grill on high with lid closed; or, if using charcoal grill, prepare for direct heat cooking over hot charcoal. If you are using a gas grill, reduce the temperature of the grill to medium-high. Carefully coat the grill surface with cooking spray, spraying at an angle.

Slice the squash lengthwise and remove seeds and loose bits. Coat with olive oil or cooking spray and place on a large piece of heavy duty tin foil. Fold up the edges to seal the squash completely. Place directly on the grill grate and cook for about 10 minutes and turn over to cook for another 6–8 minutes or until it's tender all the way through. Once done, remove from grill but keep it wrapped in foil while preparing the sauce.

To make the sauce: In a medium sauce pan, add in sauce, fresh chopped basil, parsley, Kalamata olives, and capers. Stir and cook over medium heat until it simmers.

Unwrap the squash and fluff up the flesh of cut side to release the "spaghetti-like" strands of squash. Once fluffed, top with a generous amount of sauce, sprinkle with shaved Manchego, more basil, red chili pepper flakes to taste, and fresh cracked pepper. Serve immediately!

Options: Prior to adding the sauce, add in a little grated Parmesan or more Manchego directly to the squash and fluff with a fork; then add the sauce on top.

Grilling Secret #20
Need more protein? Add cooked ground beef or ground turkey into the Puttanesca sauce.

Chapter 4

Simply Chicken

Tandoori-Style Chicken with Brown Rice and Chickpeas

Makes 4 servings.

Marinate for at least 4 hours or overnight.

For the chicken and the marinade:

4 boneless, skinless chicken breasts

1 cup plain nonfat Greek yogurt

1 tablespoon plus 2 teaspoons fresh
   lemon juice

1½ teaspoons cumin

1 clove garlic, smashed, minced

1½ tablespoons fresh ginger, grated

1 teaspoon cayenne pepper (or less
   depending on desired heat)

1½ teaspoons turmeric

Himalayan pink salt or sea salt and
   pepper to taste

For the brown rice and chickpeas:

1 cup brown rice*

2 cups water

1 can garbanzo beans, rinsed, drained

2 tablespoons spring onions, diced

1 teaspoons cilantro, roughly chopped

1 teaspoon extra virgin olive oil or
   coconut oil

Himalayan pink salt or sea salt

fresh cracked pepper to taste

Optional variation: add a teaspoon of
   Patak's Concentrated Hot Curry Paste®

*(or use 2 cups fully cooked found in the
   grocery aisle or freezer case. If used;
   skip the water from ingredient list)

In food processor or blender, combine yogurt, lemon juice, cumin, garlic, ginger, cayenne pepper, turmeric, salt, and pepper and blend until well combined. In a medium bowl or a resealable bag, add chicken and marinade and place in refrigerator for at least 3 hours, or overnight.

Preheat gas grill on high with lid closed; or if using charcoal grill, prepare for direct heat cooking over hot charcoal.

Prior to grilling, remove the chicken from the refrigerator and allow to sit at room temperature for about 5–10 minutes.

Carefully coat the grill surface with cooking spray, spraying at an angle. Add the chicken directly over heat. Cook for about 5–6 minutes a side or until internal temperature reaches 165 degrees. Remove from grill and allow to stand for about 5 minutes before serving.

To make the rice: In a medium saucepan, combine water and brown rice and bring to a boil over medium-high heat. Reduce to low heat, cover saucepan, and allow to simmer for about 35–40 minutes or until liquid is completely absorbed. Remove from heat and leave covered for about 10 minutes. Remove lid, fluff rice with fork, and add oil, garbanzo beans, green onions, and salt and pepper. Garnish with chopped cilantro.

Grilled Chicken with South Carolina Mustard BBQ Sauce

Makes 2–4 servings.

Cook these on skewers.

Marinating is not necessary but always tastes better. Make extra of this dish to use in the Chicken Wraps on the following page!

2–4 boneless, skinless chicken breasts, cut into large chunks
1½ cups store-bought South Carolina mustard barbecue sauce
metal skewers, or use wooden skewers that have been soaked in water

In a medium bowl or resealable bag, add chicken breasts and barbecue sauce and mix until well coated. Allow to marinate 30 minutes to an hour, if desired.

Grilling the Chicken: Preheat gas grill on high with lid closed; or, if using charcoal grill, prepare for direct heat cooking over hot charcoal.

Carefully coat the grill surface with cooking spray, spraying at an angle. Add the chicken directly over heat. Cook for about 5–6 minutes a side or until internal temperature reaches 165 degrees. Remove from grill and allow to stand for about 3–5 minutes before serving.

Grilling Secret #21
For extra moist and flavorful chicken, add a little bit of nonfat Greek yogurt with the South Carolina Mustard BBQ Sauce. Allow chicken to marinate overnight and you won't be disappointed.

Easy Lunch: Chicken Wraps with Healthy Slaw

Makes 2–4 servings.

Use leftovers from the Grilled Chicken recipe on page 82 to make these simple wraps.

For the wraps:

leftover cold grilled chicken with South
Carolina BBQ sauce, thinly sliced or
diced

2–4 whole wheat wraps, lavash flatbreads, or spinach quesadillas

For the slaw:

1 package broccoli slaw mix or fresh
chopped purple cabbage

¼ cup plain nonfat or Greek yogurt

¼ cup Vegenaise®, or 3 tablespoons
nonfat Greek yogurt and 2 teaspoons
organic mayonnaise

1 tablespoon apple cider vinegar

¼ teaspoon celery salt

1 teaspoon blue agave nectar or honey

1 teaspoon cracked black pepper

a few sprigs of fresh cilantro, chopped

To make the slaw: Combine all ingredients except the broccoli slaw in a medium-sized bowl. Stir with a spoon. Add broccoli slaw and stir to coat. Add more or less of seasoning to taste.

To assemble the wraps: Place wraps on cutting board. Place chicken and about 2 to 3 tablespoons of slaw in center of each wrap. Fold ends toward center of wrap and roll. Slice in half to serve.

Options: Add a little BBQ sauce as a condiment on the side.

Note: for the grilled red yams pictured here, see page 140 for the recipe.

Grilled Chicken Breast with Zesty BBQ Sauce

Makes about 2 servings of chicken and about 1 3/4 cups BBQ sauce.

2–3 boneless, skinless chicken breasts

½ cup apple cider vinegar

1 cup ketchup

2 teaspoons celery seeds

about ½ teaspoon dried red chili flakes (or to taste)

a few shakes of cayenne pepper

4 tablespoons coconut sugar, raw or turbinado sugar

1 large or 2 small bay leaves

1 tablespoons granulated onion or onion powder (not onion salt)

4 cloves garlic, smashed and minced

2 tablespoons Worcestershire sauce

1 tablespoons plus 1 ½ teaspoons mustard powder

1½ teaspoons Himalayan pink salt or sea salt

½ teaspoon fresh ginger, grated

¼ teaspoon smoked paprika

For the sauce: In a medium saucepan, combine apple cider vinegar, ketchup, celery seeds, red chili flakes, cayenne pepper, coconut sugar, bay leaves, granulated onion, garlic, Worcestershire sauce, mustard powder, sea salt, ginger, and smoked paprika. Cook over medium heat for about 5 minutes. Remove from heat, remove and discard bay leaves, and allow to cool. Can be made ahead and stored in the refrigerator for up to 5 days.

For the chicken: In a medium bowl or resealable bag, add chicken breasts and 1 cup of bbq sauce. Set aside remaining ¾ cup bbq sauce to serve with cooked chicken. Mix until chicken is well coated.

Preheat gas grill on high with lid closed; or, if using charcoal grill, prepare for direct heat cooking over hot charcoal.

Carefully coat the grill surface with cooking spray, spraying at an angle. Add the chicken directly over heat. Cook for about 5–6 minutes a side or until internal temperature reaches 165 degrees. Remove from grill and allow to stand for about 5 minutes before serving. Serve with reserved bbq sauce.

Tamarind Marinated Chicken with Goji Berry Salad

Makes 2-4 servings.

Marinate chicken at least an hour.

2–4 boneless, skinless chicken breasts

½ cup extra virgin olive oil

⅔ cup tamarind paste*

1 teaspoon cayenne pepper

1 teaspoon turmeric

1 teaspoon mild chili powder

1 clove garlic, smashed and finely
   minced

1 tablespoon blue agave nectar or honey

2 tablespoons apple cider vinegar

salt and pepper to taste

*Look for a jar of this in the Indian food
   section at the store.

In a food processor or blender, combine extra virgin olive oil, tamarind paste, cayenne pepper, turmeric, chili powder, garlic, blue agave nectar, apple cider vinegar, salt and pepper and mix until well blended. In a medium bowl or resealable bag, combine chicken breasts with marinade, mix until coated. Place in refrigerator and marinate for at least 1 hour.

Grilling the Chicken: Preheat gas grill on high with lid closed; or, if using charcoal grill, prepare for direct heat cooking over hot charcoal.

Remove chicken breasts from refrigerator and allow to stand at room temperature for 5–10 minutes prior to grilling.

Carefully coat the grill surface with cooking spray, spraying at an angle. Add the chicken directly over heat. Cook for about 5–6 minutes a side or until internal temperature reaches 165 degrees. Remove from grill and allow to stand for about 5 minutes before serving.

Side Salad idea:
swiss chard
goji berries
dried apricots, cut
slivered almonds

Dressing:
Equal parts olive oil, apple cider vinegar, and blue agave nectar or honey. Add 1 or 2 cloves of garlic, minced. Mix well.

Jerk Chicken, "Yeah Mon"

Makes 4 servings.

Traditional jerk chicken is made with whole bone-in chicken with skins left on to create a nice char. I've left the skin off to save on a little fat. This ingredient list may seem daunting to some, but many prepared store-bought jerk spices are way too salty and don't taste fresh.

Marinate chicken overnight for most robust flavor.

4 chicken breasts, skinless, boneless

Marinade:

½ cup apple cider vinegar

2–3 tablespoons water

3 tablespoons turbinado sugar or raw sugar

1 cup ketchup

½ purple onion or yellow onion, chopped fine

4–6 garlic cloves, smashed, minced

2 tablespoons thyme, fresh or dried

1 habanero chili with seeds removed, chopped fine

2 tablespoons coconut oil or grapeseed oil

3 teaspoons ground allspice

3 teaspoons ground cinnamon

3 teaspoons fresh ginger, grated fine

1–2 bay leaves, crumbled fine

½ teaspoons ground nutmeg

1 teaspoons pink salt or sea salt

2 teaspoons fresh cracked black pepper

2 limes, juiced plus lime zest

For the marinade: In a small saucepan, add apple cider vinegar, water, and sugar until sugar is dissolved. Remove from saucepan and transfer to a blender. Add all remaining marinade ingredients and blend until fairly smooth.

Preparing the chicken: Place chicken breasts on a plate and squirt lime juice on each side. Toss them in a resealable plastic bag or container and add the marinade and the lime zest. Shake bag to coat the chicken. Place in the refrigerator overnight for peak flavor.

Grilling the chicken: Preheat gas grill on high with lid closed; or, if using charcoal grill, prepare for direct heat cooking over medium-hot charcoal.

Carefully coat the grill surface with cooking spray, spraying at an angle. Add the chicken directly over heat. Brush on leftover marinade while cooking, if desired. Cook for about 5–6 minutes a side or until internal temperature reaches 165 degrees. Remove from grill and allow to stand for about 3–5 minutes before serving.

Chinese 5-Spiced Chicken with Snow Peas and Red Quinoa

Makes 2–4 servings.

Marinate at least an hour or overnight.

2–4 boneless, skinless chicken breasts
⅓ cup low sodium soy sauce
⅓ cup sesame seed oil or
    grapeseed oil
2 teaspoons rice vinegar, or seasoned
    rice vinegar
2 tablespoons Chinese 5-Spice powder
1 teaspoon ginger, freshly grated
3 garlic cloves, smashed, minced
2 teaspoons honey
a dash or 2 of cayenne pepper

Snow Peas and Red Quinoa

about 2 cups fully cooked red quinoa
    (look for this in the grocery aisle or
    freezer case fully cooked!)
1–2 tablespoons coconut oil or toasted
    sesame seed oil
1–2 spring onions, minced
2 cups fresh snow peas, or sugar snap peas
dash of pink salt or sea salt
dash of cayenne pepper
2 tablespoons rice vinegar
1 cup raw or roasted cashews, pieces
1 small can mandarin oranges (look for
    one without syrup)
a few sliced grape tomatoes (optional)

In a medium bowl, combine all ingredients for marinade. Add chicken and coat. Cover and place in refrigerator for at least an hour or overnight.

Grilling the chicken: Preheat gas grill on high with lid closed; or if using charcoal grill, prepare for direct heat cooking over hot charcoal.

Remove chicken breasts from refrigerator and allow to stand at room temperature for 5–10 minutes prior to grilling.

Carefully coat the grill surface with cooking spray, spraying at an angle. Add the chicken directly over heat. Cook for about 5–6 minutes a side or until internal temperature reaches 165 degrees.

Remove chicken from grill and allow to stand for about 5 minutes before serving with Snow Peas and Quinoa Salad.

To make the Snow Peas and Quinoa Salad, heat coconut oil in a grill-safe pan and place directly over heat (or cook inside on stove). Once hot, add in spring onions, tomatoes (if desired), snow peas, salt, and pepper. Stir and cook until snow peas are softened. Once done, transfer to a large bowl. Add in all remaining ingredients except mandarin oranges. Stir to mix seasonings. Gently add in mandarin oranges and mix. Add a few extra cashews on top for garnish if desired.

Serve warm or chilled.

Note: if you can't find fully cooked quinoa, prepare raw quinoa according to package instructions for making 2 cups.

Grilling Secret #22
For endless variations, try adding baby carrots, bamboo shoots, water chestnuts, or chopped peanuts to the salad! Make lettuce rollups with this recipe for even more crunch.

Hot Curry Chicken

Makes 4 servings.

4 chicken breasts, boneless, skinless

1 cup plain nonfat Greek yogurt

4–6 tablespoons Patak's Concentrated
Hot Curry Paste®

¼ cup water

Himalayan pink salt and pepper to taste

In food processor or blender, combine yogurt, curry paste, water, and salt, and pepper and pulse until blended. Taste test to check desired spice level for heat. Adjust if necessary.

In a medium bowl or a resealable bag, add chicken and coat with the marinade. Place in refrigerator for at least 4 hours or overnight.

Preheat gas grill on high with lid closed; or if using charcoal grill, prepare for direct heat cooking over hot charcoal.

Prior to grilling, remove the chicken from the refrigerator and allow to sit at room temperature for about 5–10 minutes.

Carefully coat the grill surface with cooking spray, spraying at an angle. Add the chicken directly over heat. Cook for about 5–6 minutes a side or until internal temperature reaches 165 degrees. Remove from grill and allow to stand for about 5 minutes before serving. Garnish with cilantro, if desired.

Blood Orange Ginger Chicken

Makes about 4 servings.

Marinate for at least an hour more.

4 boneless, skinless chicken breasts

⅓ cup fresh squeezed lime juice (about 3 limes)

2 blood oranges, juiced (or any medium sized oranges)

about 2 tablespoons fresh grated orange zest

2 cloves garlic, smashed and minced

⅓ cup orange marmalade

1 teaspoons red chili pepper flakes

¼ cup soy sauce

1 tablespoons fresh ginger, grated

To make the marinade: In a small bowl, combine lime juice, blood orange juice, orange zest, garlic, orange marmalade, red chili flakes, soy sauce, and ginger. Mix until well combined. In a medium bowl or resealable bag, add marinade and chicken breasts and place in refrigerator for 1–3 hours.

To grill the chicken: Preheat gas grill on high with lid closed; or if using charcoal grill, prepare for direct heat cooking over hot charcoal.

Remove chicken breasts from refrigerator and allow to stand at room temperature for about 5–10 minutes prior to grilling.

Carefully coat the grill surface with cooking spray, spraying at an angle. Add the chicken directly over heat. Cook for about 5–6 minutes a side or until internal temperature reaches 165 degrees. Remove from grill and allow to stand for about 5 minutes before serving.

Grilling Secret #23
Use leftovers for the salad recipe on next page!

Easy Lunch Blood Orange Ginger Chicken Salad with Curry and Blood Orange Vinaigrette

For the salad:

leftover chilled Blood Orange Ginger Chicken, sliced or diced (whatever you prefer) (page 96)

baby kale or baby spinach

goji berries

purple onion, julienne sliced

grape tomatoes sliced in half

cashew pieces or almond slivers

Tangy Curry Blood Orange Vinaigrette:

¼ cup apple cider vinegar

about 2–3 tablespoons blood orange juice, or any orange juice

2 or 3 teaspoons mild curry powder

4 tablespoons honey or blue agave nectar

2 garlic cloves, smashed, minced

2 tablespoons grape seed oil or extra virgin olive oil

dash of Himalayan pink salt or sea salt

fresh cracked pepper

To make the salad: Toss all ingredients in a bowl with the vinaigrette. Serve with chicken on the side or diced up and tossed into the salad.

To make the dressing: Mix ingredients, adding more or less of each for desired balance of tang and sweet.

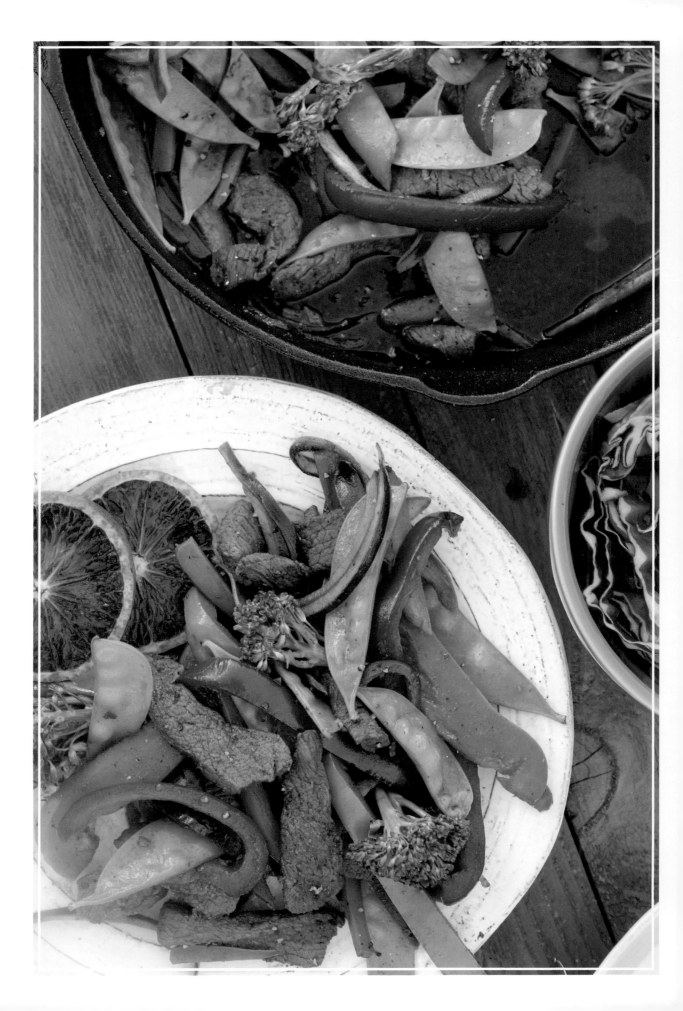

Chapter 5

Sizzling Stir-Fries and Skillet-based Grilling

Spicy Shrimp with Chili Flakes and Basil

Makes about 3 servings.

8–10 large fresh shrimp, shells removed, rinsed and patted dry (leave tails on if desired)

coconut oil or grapeseed oil

a handful of fresh sugar snap peas or snow peas

1–1½ sweet peppers, seeded and julienne cut (I used red and yellow)

½ an onion, chopped into pieces

¼ cup canned coconut milk

dash of soy sauce

about a teaspoon fresh grated ginger

2–3 garlic cloves, smashed, minced

dry Szechuan chili peppers (whole) or use slivers of red Fresno peppers, seeded, or red chili flakes

Thai basil or fresh regular basil, chopped

juice of 1 lime

Option: brown rice, freekeh, quinoa, or buckwheat noodles

Preheat gas grill on high with lid closed; or if using charcoal grill, prepare for direct heat cooking over hot charcoal.

Place an oven-safe or cast iron skillet directly on the grill grate. Heat up about 2–3 tablespoons coconut oil. Once hot, add in peas, sweet peppers, and onion and stir quickly. Add in coconut milk, soy sauce, ginger, garlic, and hot peppers. Cook for about 2–3 minutes and then toss in shrimp. Continue to stir constantly. When shrimp are opaque and firm, remove entire skillet from grill and set aside to cool. Toss in Thai basil, squeeze fresh lime over top, and serve over brown rice, freekeh, quinoa, or buckwheat noodles, if desired.

Other options to try: add diced up broccoli crowns, slices of bok choy, sliced carrots, green onions.

Grilling Secret #24

Be sure to use a cast iron or oven-safe skillet when cooking directly on the grill grate. Do not use one that has a rubber coated or wooden handle. Keep the oven mitt handy because the handle will get extremely hot.

Easy Grilled Paella

Makes 4–6 servings (depending on how hungry your guests are).

So seriously yummy . . . and so easy to make on the grill. This only takes about 30 minutes. It's awesome for a dinner party, and you can use just about any kind of seafood for this dish.

Use a paella skillet or a cast iron skillet for this recipe, if you have it.

6–8 large shrimp, shelled, rinsed, deveined if desired (leave tails on)

2–3 all natural chicken Andouille sausage links

1 cup clam juice

½ cup chicken or vegetable broth (or water)

½ cup uncooked freekeh (or rice of your choice)

6 garlic cloves, smashed and minced

⅓ cup white onion, diced

½ of a large sweet red bell pepper, sliced into strips

½ of a large yellow or orange bell pepper, sliced into strips

2 pinches of saffron (about ½ teaspoon)

cayenne pepper

1 tomato, cored and diced

1 cup fresh or frozen peas

4–5 fresh clams or mussels, rinsed and scrubbed

fresh flat-leaf parsley

2 lemons, sliced into wedges, seeded

sea salt or pink sat and fresh cracked pepper to taste

grapeseed oil or olive oil

about ¼ cup of water

Preheat gas grill on high with lid closed; or if using charcoal grill, prepare for direct heat cooking over hot charcoal. Spray or brush the grill grate with a little cooking oil. Add the andouille sausage and cook for about 7–8 minutes, turning once, or until the internal temperature reaches 145 degrees. Remove from grill. Transfer to a cutting board and cut links at a diagonal. Set aside.

Heat paella skillet or cast iron skillet directly on the grill grate. Once heated, add clam juice and broth. Add the freekeh or rice, garlic, onions, and peppers. Stir. Add in saffron and a few shakes of cayenne pepper. Close lid and let simmer about 10 minutes. The grill temperature should be about 400–500 degrees.

Open grill lid, add in tomato and sliced sausage and stir. Close lid again and cook for about another 5 minutes.

Open lid and stir again; the freekeh should have absorbed most of the liquid by now. Add in raw shrimp and cook about 5 minutes. Add in fresh or frozen peas and the clams or mussels. Add in a few cranks of fresh ground salt. Because cooking temperatures may vary, water may be necessary to add to the skillet so it's not too dry. Add in about ¼ cup or ½ cup, if desired. Close the lid and cook for another 2–3 minutes.

Paella is done when the shrimp are firm and pink, and the clams and/or mussels are opened. Remove skillet from heat and allow to rest about 5 minutes. Toss in parsley and fresh squeezed lemon. Serve with additional wedges of lemon.

Flank Steak with Broccoli and Red Pepper

Makes 4 servings.

This one's better if allowed to marinate for at least 2 hours.

For the steak marinade:

1 pound flank steak, or other cut of beef like tri-tip or round

2 tablespoons low sodium soy sauce

2 teaspoons coconut sugar or turbinado sugar

about a teaspoon of fresh grated ginger

2–3 large garlic cloves, smashed and minced

2 tablespoons seasoned rice vinegar (or unseasoned is fine too)

a few dashes of white pepper

For the veggies:

1 teaspoon mushroom soy or dark soy (if you can find it; if not, skip it)

3 teaspoons toasted sesame seed oil or coconut oil

2 cups fresh broccoli florets

1 cup sugar snap peas

1 red bell pepper, cored and seeded, julienne cut

¼ cup cashew pieces (raw unsalted preferred)

1 small onion, julienne cut

Slice the flank steak across the grain into thin ¼-inch wide strips, each about 3 inches long. Toss marinade ingredients together with steak in an airtight container and mix together to coat. Place in refrigerator for at least 2 hours. Trust me, it is worth the wait!

Remove marinated beef from the refrigerator and let stand at room temperature about 30 minutes.

Preheat gas grill on high with lid closed; or if using charcoal grill, prepare for direct heat cooking over hot charcoal. If you are using a gas grill, reduce the temperature of the grill to medium-high.

Heat up a cast iron skillet or oven safe skillet directly on the grill. Once heated, add the coconut oil or toasted sesame seed oil and toss in the beef. Stir constantly about 3–4 minutes until browned. Once done, remove beef and set aside. Add in all veggies and sauce ingredients to the same skillet and cook for about 3–4 minutes, stirring constantly. Once broccoli is slightly tender add beef back into the skillet and cook for about 1 minute. Mix thoroughly and carefully remove skillet from heat. Serve on top of your favorite rice, quinoa, or freekeh.

Green Cauliflower with garlic, Parmesan, and Sumac

Makes 3–4 servings.

1–2 heads of green cauliflower or
    broccoli flower, cut into steaks about ½
    inch thick

¼ cup grated parmesan cheese

1 teaspoon sumac

4–5 cloves garlic, smashed, minced

fresh cracked pepper

sea salt or pink salt to taste

grapeseed oil or cooking spray

dash or two of red chili flakes

teaspoon of butter or Earth Balance®

fresh diced basil for garnish (optional)

Preheat gas grill on high with lid closed; or if using charcoal grill, prepare for direct heat cooking over hot charcoal.

Take cauliflower and spray or coat with oil and place in a bowl. Add in sumac, garlic, pepper, salt, and red chili flakes. Stir to coat.

Place an oven-safe or cast iron skillet directly on the grill grate. Heat up about 2–3 tablespoons of oil. Once the skillet and oil is heated, add the cauliflower. Cover and cook about 10–12 minutes, stirring several times. If it's starting to burn, add a little water to the skillet. Once fork tender, add in parmesan cheese and butter or Earth Balance. Stir. Remove from heat and serve.

Grill Secret #25
Try this with yellow or purple cauliflower or all 3 kinds together!
Works great with broccoli too! If you wish to make this vegan, skip the parmesan cheese and use nutritional yeast instead.

Grilled Sauteed Kale with Peanut Dressing and Sprouted Jasmine Rice

Makes 3–4 servings.

Use a cast iron skillet or oven-safe skillet for this recipe.

1 pound of kale, any kind (I used curly green and curly purple kale), rinsed and de-veined

2 tablespoons coconut oil

1 cup carrots, julienne cut

2 large garlic cloves, smashed and minced

½ cup slivered almonds or peanuts

1 package fully cooked store-bought sprouted jasmine rice*

sesame seeds for garnish, if desired

*Look for sprouted jasmine rice in the grocery aisle in gusset bags or substitute fully cooked brown rice.

For the dressing:

¼ cup San-J Thai Peanut Sauce®, or other store-bought peanut sauce

for extra zing, add a tablespoon of rice vinegar

dash or 2 of cayenne pepper

Preheat gas grill on high with lid closed; or if using charcoal grill, prepare for direct heat cooking over hot charcoal.

While the grill is heating up, devein the leaves of kale by taking a sharp knife along the stem and slice off the vein on both sides. Discard the vein and stem. Chop the remaining leaves into about 2-inch pieces.

Place an oven-safe or cast iron skillet directly on the grill grate. Heat up about 2 tablespoons of oil. Once the skillet and oil is heated, add carrots. Stir constantly for a few minutes until slightly tender, then add kale and garlic. Continue to stir constantly. Once tender, turn heat down and add dressing and nuts. Reduce heat to low and cook a few more minutes until kale and carrots are tender. Remove and serve with fully cooked sprouted basmati or jasmine rice or your favorite grain. Either stir rice and kale mixture together or serve veggies on top of rice.

Chicken in White Wine with Porcini Mushrooms, Asparagus, and Asiago Cheese

Makes 4 servings.

2 chicken breasts, boneless, skinless, cut into strips

½ cup asiago cheese, grated

6–8 pieces of asparagus, cut into bite-sized pieces

6 tablespoons butter

⅔ cup dry white wine

½ cup of dried porcini mushrooms, reconstituted in warm water

3–4 leaves fresh sage, minced

about ½ teaspoon fresh thyme leaves

a few grape or cherry tomatoes, grilled

grapeseed oil

fresh black pepper or whole green peppercorns

a few leaves of fresh basil

dash of Himalayan pink salt

Preheat gas grill on high with lid closed; or if using charcoal grill, prepare for direct heat cooking over hot charcoal.

While the grill is heating up, slice the chicken and grate the cheese. Place chicken on a plate and add salt and pepper to coat.

Coat asparagus with a little cooking oil and place directly on the grill grate using tongs. Cook until tender, turning once or twice, then set aside.

Place an oven-safe or cast iron skillet directly on the grill grate. Heat up about 2 tablespoons of oil. Once hot and slightly smoking, add chicken and sauté until brown, about 4 minutes. Add in a little butter, white wine, and all other ingredients except cheese. Stir and cook for about 2 minutes. Then add grated cheese and stir. Toss in grilled tomatoes, and chopped basil. Carefully remove skillet using an oven mitt. Serve family-style in the skillet.

Grilling Secret #26
Leave the lid off for this recipe and keep stirring. Make variations of this dish using zucchini, or use Marsala wine instead of white wine for a slightly sweeter and more savory dish. Try morel mushrooms instead of porcini.

Garlicky Shrimp with Smoked Paprika and Peas

Makes 3-4 servings.

1 lb of medium or large shrimp, shelled
and deveined

2–3 teaspoons extra virgin olive oil

½–¾ teaspoon smoked paprika

1 pinch of saffron

6–8 large garlic cloves, smashed and
minced

1 teaspoon ketchup

¼ cup onion, diced fine

1½ teaspoons butter or ghee

2–3 tablespoons water

½ cup frozen peas, thawed slightly or
fresh peas

a few sprigs of fresh parsley, chopped

squeeze of fresh lemon

dash or 2 of fresh cracked pepper

Option: serve over noodles

Preheat gas grill on high with lid closed; or if using charcoal grill, prepare for direct heat cooking over hot charcoal.

While the grill is heating up, devein shrimp, rinse, and pat dry. Place in a bowl with smoked paprika, saffron, garlic, ketchup, and a dash or two of salt and pepper.

Place an oven-safe or cast iron skillet directly on the grill grate. Heat up about 2 tablespoons of oil. Once skillet and oil are hot, add in onion and shrimp. Stir rapidly and continue to cook for about 2 minutes. Add in butter, spices, ketchup, and a little water. Add in peas and stir until shrimp are opaque and firm, and the onions are tender and translucent. Continue to cook a minute or 2 more and remove from heat. Finish with fresh squeezed lemon. Add parsley and serve as is or over noodles of your choice.

Grilled Spicy Skillet Cornbread

Makes 6–8 slices.

1 egg

¼ cup grapeseed oil or vegetable oil

1¼ cups water

2½ cups Bob's Cornbread Muffin Mix®

1 red Fresno pepper, seeded and
  chopped (or jalepeno pepper)

½ sweet red bell pepper, seeded and
  chopped

1 poblano pepper, seeded and chopped

¼ cup asiago or cheddar cheese, grated

dash of salt

1 tablespoon plus 1 teaspoon blue agave
  nectar or honey

Preheat gas grill on high with lid closed; or if using charcoal grill, prepare for direct heat cooking over hot charcoal.

Mix all ingredients together with a spoon—not an electric mixer.

Generously spray a cast iron skillet or oven-safe skillet with cooking spray. Add batter and place skillet directly on preheated grill. Close lid and cook for about 15 minutes or until done. To check to see if cornbread is done, insert a wooden skewer in the center of the skillet; if it comes out dry and clean, the bread is done. Remove from heat and set aside to cool slightly before slicing and removing bread from skillet.

Chapter 6

For the Love of Veggies

Grilled Spaghetti Squash with Sage and Parmesan Cheese

Makes 2 servings (depending on size of spaghetti squash).

1 large spaghetti squash, sliced in half

½ purple onion

2 tablespoons butter or Earth
   Balance Buttery Spread®

parmesan cheese, shaved

6–7 fresh sage leaves

sea salt or pink salt to taste

fresh cracked pepper

Grilling the squash: Preheat gas grill on high with lid closed; or if using charcoal grill, prepare for direct heat cooking over hot charcoal. If you are using a gas grill, reduce the temperature of the grill to medium-high. Carefully coat the grill surface with cooking spray, spraying at an angle.

Slice the squash lengthwise and remove seeds and loose bits. Coat with olive oil or cooking spray and place on a large piece of heavy duty tin foil and fold up the edges to seal the squash completely. Place directly on the grill grate and cook for about 10 minutes. Turn over to cook for another 6–8 minutes or until it's tender all the way through. Once done, remove from grill but keep it wrapped in foil while preparing the sauce.

While the squash is cooking, slice the onion into about ½-inch thick discs. Coat with a little cooking oil and place directly on grill grate for 2–3 minutes per side or until tender. Once done, remove from grill and transfer to a cutting board to cool. Dice into pieces and set aside.

When the squash is done, remove from grill and fluff the squash with a fork. Add about a tablespoon of butter per side of squash, salt and pepper to taste. Add in parmesan to taste, diced sage leaves, and the onions. Sprinkle a few more shavings of parmesan on top and, if desired, add a few sage leaves for garnish.

Serve immediately.

Grilled Nachos with Soy Chorizo Sausage and Pico de Gallo

Makes enough for about 3–4 people.

Regular chorizo sausage usually comes with a pork casing to hold it together into links. However, soy chorizo often comes wrapped in a plastic liner—make sure you use the kind that does not have this. If you can't find soy chorizo sausage, look for vegetarian andouille sausage links instead, or Mexican seasoned soy crumbles. All these items can be found in the refrigerator case near the hummus.

1 large bag blue corn chips (or any kind of tortilla chips)

1 can aduki beans or black beans, rinsed and drained

sweet baby peppers, sliced

about 1 cup soy chorizo sausage, diced or crumbled (depending on which brand you get)

about 1 cup queso fresco, crumbled

1 avocado, sliced in half, with skin on and seed removed

lime

cooking spray

tin foil and grilling tray

For the Pico De Gallo:

fresh cilantro, diced, for garnish

1 large jalapeño, seeded and diced

3–4 large garlic cloves, smashed and minced

3 large tomatoes, diced

2–3 limes, juiced

1 medium red or white onion, diced fine

sea salt or pink salt to taste

Preheat gas grill on high with lid closed; or if using charcoal grill, prepare for direct heat cooking over hot charcoal. If you are using a gas grill, reduce the temperature of the grill to medium-high. Carefully coat the grill surface with cooking spray, spraying at an angle.

Cover a grilling tray with tin foil. Place a layer of corn chips on top. Sprinkle beans, peppers, and soy chorizo sausage on top of corn chips. Sprinkle with a little queso fresco. Place on the grill and close the lid for about 6–10 minutes on medium heat. While the nachos are cooking, place avocado slices directly on the grill for 1–2 minutes with flesh side down Remove nachos and avocado from grill. Add fresh squeezed lime over avocado with a little salt.

In a bowl mix all the pico de gallo ingredients together. This tastes even better if you can allow this to sit for a few hours to flavor up prior to serving.

Pour pico de gallo over top of nachos and serve immediately.

Grilled Kabocha Squash with Chipotle and Cotija Cheese

Makes 3–4 servings, depending on size of squash.

1 medium to large Kabocha squash

2–3 teaspoons chipotle powder

Cotija cheese, crumbled

fresh cilantro, chopped, for garnish

sea salt or pink salt to taste

cooking spray or extra virgin olive oil

Preheat gas grill on high with lid closed; or if using charcoal grill, prepare for direct heat cooking over hot charcoal. If you are using a gas grill, reduce the temperature of the grill to medium-high. Carefully coat the grill surface with cooking spray, spraying at an angle.

To cut the squash: Starting near the right of the stem at the top of the squash, with a sharp knife pierce the skin of the squash and cut down through the center, creating two halves. Scoop out the seeds and fibers with a spoon. While holding one side of the squash, slice thin wedges about ½ an inch thick (or thicker if desired). Leave skins on if desired.

Brush or spray cooking oil on the wedges on both sides. Sprinkle with salt and chipotle powder.

Place directly on the grill and cook about 3–5 minutes on each side or until tender.

Once done, remove from grill and place on serving platter. Sprinkle with Cotija cheese and fresh diced cilantro. Serve immediately.

Note: If you can't find Cotija cheese, you can use queso fresco.

Easy Grilled Summer Squash with Honey Mustard

Makes about 4 servings.

2 medium to large zucchini squash,
   sliced diagonally into pieces about
   ¼-inch thick

2–3 medium yellow squash, sliced
   diagonally into pieces about ¼–inch
   thick

1 cup store-bought honey mustard
   (without wine)

2 teaspoons apple cider vinegar

2 teaspoons fresh or dried thyme

fresh cracked pepper

sea salt or pink salt to taste

Preheat gas grill on high with lid closed; or if using charcoal grill, prepare for direct heat cooking over hot charcoal. If you are using a gas grill, reduce the temperature of the grill to medium-high. Carefully coat the grill surface with cooking spray, spraying at an angle.

In a large bowl, combine all ingredients and stir to coat vegetables.

Place directly on the grill or use a grill grate. Cook about 3–4 minutes per side and remove from grill.

The "Emily Burger"—Best Ever Vegan Burger

Makes 4–5 servings.

This recipe was inspired by my friend Emily Duke's recipe for her vegan wheat berry burger.

¾ cup red onion, chopped fine

2 tablespoons garlic, chopped

1 carrot, grated

¾ cup frozen spinach, thawed, strained, and chopped (or about 1 ½ cups fresh, chopped)

2 cups fully cooked lentils (look for Melissa's Produce® fully cooked lentils in the produce department)

1½ cups quinoa, fully cooked (or look for fully cooked black barley, red quinoa and brown rice in the freezer case)

2 tablespoons ground flax seeds + 2 tablespoons water

1 cups whole wheat bread crumbs

⅓ cup nutritional yeast

1 tablespoon Old Bay Seasoning®

1 tablespoon garlic powder

⅓ cup arrowroot powder (or corn starch)

1 cup raw or roasted walnuts, chopped

fresh cracked pepper and Himalayan pink salt to taste

a few shakes of cayenne pepper

Optional toppings: Vegenaise®, ketchup, bibb lettuce, sliced tomato

Optional: add 1–2 tablespoons extra virgin olive oil

In a skillet, add onion, garlic, carrots, and spinach to about a teaspoon of olive oil. Stir and cook over medium heat until veggies are tender.

In a large bowl, combine cooked vegetables with remaining ingredients and stir together. If mixture is too dry, add 1–2 tablespoons of extra virgin olive oil.

Preparing and grilling the burgers: Preheat gas grill on high with lid closed; or if using charcoal grill, prepare for direct heat cooking over hot charcoal. If you are using a gas grill, reduce the temperature of the grill to medium-high. Carefully coat the grill surface with cooking spray, spraying at an angle.

While the grill is heating up, carefully form 4-ounce patties (about the size of your palm). Keep hands wet while working so they don't stick. Brush or spray cooking oil to both sides of each burger and place directly on the grill. Cook about 4–5 minutes per side. Serve with Vegenaise® mixed with a little Old Bay® seasoning on top of fresh bibb lettuce, sliced tomato, and sweet or purple onion.

Note: you can also use canned lentils, rinsed, drained, and patted dry.

For a non-vegan version of this same recipe, substitute nutritional yeast with grated Parmesan cheese and a few shakes of cayenne pepper.

Zucchini Rollup Appetizers with Smoked Paprika Hummus

Makes about 5 rollups for each medium zucchini.

3–4 zucchini

1 small container store-bought hummus, plain or garlic

2 teaspoons fresh squeezed lemon juice

about a teaspoon smoked paprika

fire-roasted or sundried tomatoes (the kind found on salad bars or jars in olive oil)

toothpicks

cooking spray

For the hummus: In a medium-sized bowl, combine hummus, lemon juice, and smoked paprika and stir together.

For the zucchini: Preheat gas grill on high with lid closed; or if using charcoal grill, prepare for direct heat cooking over hot charcoal. If you are using a gas grill, reduce the temperature of the grill to medium-high. Carefully coat the grill surface with cooking spray, spraying at an angle.

While the grill is heating up, carefully slice zucchini lengthwise into ¼-inch strips, leaving skin on.

Brush olive oil or spray cooking oil on zucchini strips. Place directly on grill to cook about 4 minutes, turning once. When they are slightly tender, remove from grill to cool.

Once zucchini have cooled, add about 1½ tablespoons of hummus mixture to the edge of a zucchini strip and roll up. Place a toothpick through the hummus to keep zucchini together. Place directly on serving tray. Garnish each rollup with a slice or 2 of fire-roasted tomatoes. Rollups can be served chilled or at room temperature.

Grilled Yams with Black Rice and Goat Cheese

Makes about 8–10 pieces.

2 large red yams, scrubbed with skins left on and sliced into ½–¾-inch thick discs
1 cup vegetable broth or water
½ cup black rice (also called Forbidden Rice or mahogany rice)
About ½ cup crumbled goat cheese

In a saucepan on your kitchen stove, bring vegetable broth to a boil over high heat. Rinse black rice in cold water and drain. Add rice to boiling water, cover, and reduce heat to simmer for about 20–25 minutes or until tender. Once done, set aside.

Preheat gas grill on high with lid closed; or if using charcoal grill, prepare for direct heat cooking over hot charcoal. If you are using a gas grill, reduce the temperature of the grill to medium-high. Carefully coat the grill surface with cooking spray, spraying at an angle.

Brush or spray yams with cooking spray or olive oil. Place directly on the grill and cook for about 5–6 minutes, turning once. Once they are fork tender, remove them from the grill. Place directly on plate. With a spoon, pile rice on top of each piece. Top with about a teaspoon of goat cheese and serve immediately.

Options: if desired, you can also leave the yams on grill when topping with rice and goat cheese to melt the cheese before serving.

Leaning Tower of Eggplant

Makes about 2 or 3 stacks.

1 large eggplant

4 large cloves garlic, smashed and
   minced

¼ cup extra virgin olive oil or
   grapeseed oil

1 large purple onion

1 medium zucchini

1 yellow bell pepper

1 red bell pepper

1 large portobello mushroom cap

sea salt and fresh black pepper to taste.

pesto (see page 62 for recipe, or use
   store-bought pesto)

crumbled feta cheese

diced basil for garnish (optional)

Before heating grill, add garlic to olive oil and allow to flavor up for about 30 minutes at room temperature. This will make the oil very peppery and yummy.

Preheat gas grill on high with lid closed; or if using charcoal grill, prepare for direct heat cooking over hot charcoal. If you are using a gas grill, reduce the temperature of the grill to medium-high. Carefully coat the grill surface with cooking spray, spraying at an angle.

Remove stem from portobello and slice eggplant and onions into discs that are about ⅜ to ½-inch thick. Make sure to keep the onions intact. Slice the zucchini into lengthwise strips that are about ⅜-inch thick. Slice the peppers into wide strips and remove seeds and stem.

Place all vegetables in a bowl and toss in olive oil and garlic, salt, and pepper to coat; or simply brush on or spray on oil to coat.

Place directly on grill and cook all vegetables until tender, about 3–5 minutes, turning once while cooking.

Once vegetables are tender, remove from grill and stack according to your preference. Take a look at the photo for some suggestions on plating. Top with a decent amount of fresh pesto, and add crumbled feta on top. Hit with some additional fresh cracked pepper.

Grilled Carrots with Za'atar and Goat Cheese

Makes 2 servings (2–3 carrots per person).

6 whole carrots, peeled

2–3 tablespoons extra virgin olive oil

fresh cracked pepper

sea salt or pink salt

about 2 teaspoons Za'atar seasoning

dash of cayenne pepper (optional, but yummy)

crumbled goat cheese

Preheat gas grill on high with lid closed; or if using charcoal grill, prepare for direct heat cooking over hot charcoal. If you are using a gas grill, reduce the temperature of the grill to medium-high. Carefully coat the grill surface with cooking spray, spraying at an angle.

In a small bowl, mix together olive oil and seasonings. Toss in carrots to coat evenly.

Grill carrots over about 400–500 degree heat, turning them every 3–4 minutes, taking care not to char them too much. If they are cooking too fast, turn the temperature down (if it's a gas grill) or move them away from the coals if using a charcoal grill. Carrots should take about 15–25 minutes to cook and get tender, depending on size.

Once carrots are tender, remove from grill and place on serving tray. Top with crumbled goat cheese.

Grilled Flatbread Appetizer with Artichoke Mustard Spread

Makes 1 large flatbread (about 4 servings).

1 large or 2 small multigrain lavash flatbread wraps (or your favorite 9-inch tortilla wrap)

4 tablespoons good quality Dijon mustard

¼ cup Vegenaise® or mayonnaise

1 lemon, juiced

⅓ cup grated parmesan cheese

2 large garlic cloves, smashed and minced

½ teaspoon horseradish (optional)

1 purple onion, sliced into ⅜-inch discs

1 large 12-ounce jar of marinated artichoke hearts, plus the liquid from the jar

3–4 large leaves rainbow chard, chopped

fresh cracked pepper

Preheat gas grill on high with lid closed; or if using charcoal grill, prepare for direct heat cooking over hot charcoal. If you are using a gas grill, reduce the temperature of the grill to medium-high. Carefully coat the grill surface with cooking spray, spraying at an angle.

In a small bowl, mix together mustard, Veganaise ®, lemon juice, parmesan cheese, garlic, horseradish (if using), and fresh cracked pepper. Then set aside.

Coat the onion pieces with oil and place directly on grill, cooking about 5–6 minutes and turning once. Remove from grill as soon as they are tender.

Spray or coat lavash flatbread with a little cooking oil or olive oil and place directly on the grill for about 1 minute on each side until it gets firm and crisp. Once done, remove from grill and place on serving platter. Coat 1 side with the mustard spread. If desired, add artichokes directly from can, or grill them before topping flatbread. Top with the grilled onion and a bit more fresh lemon if desired. Sprinkle with rainbow chard and serve immediately.

Sweet and Spicy Grilled Tomatillo Salsa

Makes about 3 cups.

Do yourself a favor—make this a day ahead and it will be all flavored up for ya!

2½ cups tomatillos, whole with husks removed, rinsed clean

2 corn cobs, husks still on, to make about 1½ cups (or look for fire-roasted corn in your freezer case)

2 teaspoons warm water

2 teaspoons coconut sugar, or turbinado sugar

½ cup red onion, finely diced

5 tablespoons fresh lime juice

1 cup chopped fresh cilantro

4 tablespoons fresh garlic, smashed, minced

1 large jalapeño, seeded, minced

1 red serrano chili pepper, seeded, minced

1 teaspoon sea salt or pink salt

Preheat gas grill on high with lid closed; or if using charcoal grill, prepare for direct heat cooking over hot charcoal. If you are using a gas grill, reduce the temperature of the grill to medium-high. Carefully coat the grill surface with cooking spray, spraying at an angle.

Place the whole tomatillos directly on the grill and cook for about 2–3 minutes, turning occasionally. Once the tomatillos are charred and turn from a bright green olive green, they are done. Remove from grill and set aside to cool.

For the corn, pull back the husks and pull out the silk as much as possible, then pull the husks back over top of the corn. Place the corn directly on the grill until completely charred. Once done, remove and allow to cool enough for you to handle them. Pull the burnt husks and any remaining silks off. Place the corn vertically on a cutting board and cut the kernels from the cob on all sides.

Add warm water and sugar together and stir until dissolved.

Place all ingredients except the corn and minced red onion in a food processor and pulse until blended into a chunky purée. Once done, place in a bowl and stir in corn and minced onion. Add more lime or salt as desired. Serve with your favorite tortilla chips.

Options: Try this on top of the grilled mojito salmon on page 182.

Grilled Heirloom Potatoes with Rosemary and Garlic

Makes 4 servings.

3–4 cups whole heirloom potatoes, scrubbed, skins on

2 large garlic cloves, smashed and minced

2–3 tablespoons fresh rosemary, minced

2 teaspoons extra virgin olive oil or grapeseed oil

fresh cracked black pepper

sea salt or pink salt

tin foil

Add garlic and rosemary to oil and marinate for at least 30 minutes prior to grilling.

Preheat gas grill on high with lid closed; or if using charcoal grill, prepare for direct heat cooking over hot charcoal. If you are using a gas grill, reduce the temperature of the grill to medium-high. Carefully coat the grill surface with cooking spray, spraying at an angle.

In a bowl, mix all ingredients including the garlicky herbed oil. Stir to coat.

Tear off 2 large pieces of tin foil. Separate potatoes into two piles, one on each piece of foil. Fold up sides and make a tight ball. Place directly on the grill and close lid. Cook potatoes about 20–25 minutes, turning 2 or 3 times while cooking. Check for tenderness with a fork or knife poked into them.

Once tender, remove from grill and discard foil. Serve immediately.

Grilled Brussels Sprouts with Maple Syrup and Balsamic

Makes 4 servings.

4 cups fresh brussels sprouts, rinsed and
  dried

5 tablespoons balsamic vinegar

3 tablespoons maple syrup or blue agave
  nectar

a drizzle of olive oil or grapeseed oil

sea salt or pink salt to taste

fresh cracked pepper

tin foil

Preheat gas grill on high with lid closed; or if using charcoal grill, prepare for direct heat cooking over hot charcoal. If you are using a gas grill, reduce the temperature of the grill to medium-high. Carefully coat the grill surface with cooking spray, spraying at an angle.

Cut stems of brussels sprouts then slice in half. Place in a large bowl with remaining ingredients and stir to coat thoroughly.

Place tin foil directly on the grill grate. Spread Brussels sprouts evenly on top.

Cook them for about 15–18 minutes, carefully turning once or twice with long tongs. Once they are charred and tender, remove from the grill and serve.

Chapter 7

The Meat of the Matter

Pork Tenderloin with Garam Masala and Mango Chutney

Makes about 4 servings.

Serously simple. If you want, you can add the rub to the meat ahead of time or just before grilling.

1½–2 lbs pork tenderloin

1½ tablespoons garam masala

2 teaspoons cumin, ground

¼ teaspoon garlic powder

2 teaspoons coconut sugar

1 tablespoon extra virgin olive oil

a dash or two of Himalayan pink salt

Options for condiment: Major Grey's Hot Mango Chutney®

Mix seasonings together and set aside.

Rub pork tenderloin with about 1 tablespoon of extra virgin olive oil and apply the dry rub to all sides.

Grilling the tenderloin: Preheat gas grill on high with lid closed; or if using charcoal grill, prepare for direct heat cooking over hot charcoal.

Carefully coat the grill surface with cooking spray, spraying at an angle. Add the pork tenderloin directly over heat. With grill lid closed, cook on each side for about 8–10 minutes or until internal temperature reaches 145 degrees. Remove from heat and let pork tenderloins stand for about 5 minutes before serving.

Slice and serve with chutney.

Flank Steak with Chimichurri Sauce

Makes about 4–6 servings.

Marinate the flank steak at least 3 hours or overnight.

For flank steak and marinade:

About 1½ lbs flank steak, grass-fed if you
   can find it

juice of 2 whole lemons

4 teaspoons cumin, ground

4 tablespoons honey

1 teaspoons red pepper flakes

6 teaspoons minced garlic

4 tablespoons minced shallots

For Chimichurri Sauce:

½ cup cilantro

½ cup parsley

3 tablespoons red wine vinegar

2 teaspoons red pepper flakes

½ cup extra virgin olive oil

3 tablespoons fresh oregano, minced

6 cloves garlic

2 tablespoons lime juice, freshly
   squeezed

2 tablespoons shallots

Marinating the flank steak: Combine lemon juice, cumin, honey, red pepper flakes, minced garlic, and minced shallots. Add marinade to a medium bowl or resealable bag and add flank steak. Mix to coat thoroughly. Store in refrigerator for at least 3 hours or overnight.

You can make the chimichurri in advance and store in the refrigerator for up to 4 days. In a food processor, combine cilantro, parsley, red wine vinegar, red pepper flakes, extra virgin olive oil, oregano, garlic cloves, lime juice, and shallots. Pulse until ingredients are well mixed. After chimichurri is mixed together, taste to determine if additional red pepper flakes or lime juice are needed.

Preheat gas grill on high with lid closed; or if using charcoal grill, prepare for direct heat cooking over hot charcoal.

Prior to grilling, remove the flank steak from the refrigerator and allow to sit at room temperature for about 15 minutes.

Carefully coat the grill surface with cooking spray, spraying at an angle. Add the flank steak directly over heat. Cook for about 5–6 minutes a side or until internal temperature reaches 145 degrees. If you prefer a rare or medium rare steak, cook for about 3–5 minutes a side or until internal temperature reaches 135 degrees. Remove from grill and allow steak to stand for about 5 minutes before serving. Serve with a generous portion of chimichurri sauce.

Note: this makes just enough chimichurri for about 1½ lbs of meat.

Double the recipe if you want leftover sauce to top corn or other side dishes.

Tri-tip Steak with Sumac and a Side of Yams

Makes about 4 servings.

Sumac is a berry originating in the Middle East. It's a wonderful red berry with a lovely lemony taste and is available ground for cooking. It adds a nice acidity to all kinds of meats and vegetables. Use it on grilled carrots and sprinkle it on hummus. Sumac spice found in stores should not to be confused with the sumac plants that grow in ditches on the side of the road in North America—that variety is highly poisonous.

Marinate the tri-tip at least 3 hours or overnight.

About 1 lb of tri-tip steak, grass-fed
  preferred

¼ cup extra virgin olive oil

1 tablespoon oregano, dried

1 bunch flat-leaf parsley, washed and pat
  dried with stems removed

6 cloves garlic, smashed and minced

2 teaspoons Himalayan pink salt, ground

3–4 cranks of fresh black pepper

⅓ cup purple onion, diced

1 tablespoon white balsamic vinegar

2 teaspoons lemon juice

¼ teaspoon lemon zest

1 tablespoon sumac

Yams with Black Rice and Goat Cheese
  (page 134)

In a food processor, combine extra virgin olive oil, dried oregano, parsley, garlic cloves, salt, pepper, diced purple onion, white balsamic vinegar, lemon juice, lemon zest, and sumac. Pulse until all ingredients are well mixed. Pour marinade into a medium bowl or resealable bag and add tri-tip. Marinate in refrigerator for at least 3 hours or overnight.

Preheat gas grill on high with lid closed; or if using charcoal grill, prepare for direct heat cooking over hot charcoal.

Prior to grilling, remove tri-tip from the refrigerator and allow to sit at room temperature for about 15 minutes.

Carefully coat the grill surface with cooking spray, spraying at an angle. Add tri-tip directly over heat. With grill lid open, cook for about 4–5 minutes a side or until internal temperature reaches 145 degrees. Remove from grill and allow tri-tip to stand for about 5 minutes before serving. Serve with a side of Yams with Black Rice and Goat Cheese (page 134).

Curried Steak with Brown Rice Salad

Makes about 4–6 servings.

Marinate top sirloin steak at least 3 hours or overnight.

For the steak:

About 1½ lbs top sirloin, grass-fed
  preferred

1 cup plain nonfat or Greek yogurt

1 tablespoon yellow or white onion,
  minced

2 teaspoons mild curry powder

1 teaspoon cumin, ground

½ teaspoon garlic powder

1 teaspoon paprika

4 tablespoons grapeseed oil or extra
  virgin olive oil

⅓ cup water

1 teaspoon sea salt or pink salt

1–2 dashes cayenne pepper

For the salad:

1 lb package fully cooked brown rice
  (I used fully cooked brown jasmine
  rice—look for it in the grocery aisle)

1 large red yam, diced with skins left on

1½ cup frozen peas, thawed

1 cup dried cranberries

a few teaspoons of fresh cut cilantro

2 teaspoons mild or medium curry
  powder

drizzle of extra virgin olive oil

piece of tin foil

a few teaspoons of roasted salted pepita
  seeds (optional)

In a food processor, combine yogurt, minced onion, curry powder, cumin, garlic powder, paprika, grapeseed oil, water, salt, and cayenne pepper. Pulse until ingredients are well mixed. Pour marinade into medium bowl or resealable bag and add top sirloin. Marinate in refrigerator for at least 3 hours or overnight.

Preheat gas grill on high with lid closed; or if using charcoal grill, prepare for direct heat cooking over hot charcoal.

Prior to grilling, remove top sirloin from refrigerator and allow to sit at room temperature for about 15 minutes.

Carefully coat the grill surface with cooking spray, spraying at an angle. Add top sirloin directly over heat. With grill lid open, cook for about 4–5 minutes a side or until internal temperature reaches 145 degrees. Remove from grill and allow top sirloin to stand for about 5 minutes before serving.

For a variations on the marinade, try using garam masala instead of mild curry powder and skip the paprika.

For Brown Rice Salad: Place diced yams in the middle of a piece of tin foil. Coat with a little cooking spray and close up foil to make a packet. Place directly on the grill grate and cook at medium-high heat, turning a few times until tender, about 6–8 minutes. Once done, remove and set aside.

In a large bowl, combine all salad ingredients and mix together with a spoon. Add more seasoning to taste. Serve at room temperature, topped with the grilled steak.

Grilled Steak Salad

Makes about 2–4 servings.

For the steak:
1–2 rib eye steaks, grass-fed preferred
  (or substitute your favorite cut of meat)
extra virgin olive oil
Himalayan pink salt and fresh ground
  black pepper

For the salad:
baby mixed greens
sliced tart apples
dried cranberries
roasted pepita seeds
dressing (recipe below)
crumbled goat cheese

For salad dressing:
½ cup extra virgin olive oil,
½ cup white balsamic vinegar
1 garlic clove, smashed, minced

Option: Sprinkle some sumac in with
  your salad and on the meat.

Preheat gas grill on high with lid closed; or if using charcoal grill, prepare for direct heat cooking over hot charcoal.

Drizzle steaks with extra virgin olive oil and sprinkle both sides with salt and pepper.

Carefully coat the grill surface with cooking spray, spraying at an angle. Add rib eyes directly over heat. With grill lid open, cook for about 4–5 minutes a side or until internal temperature reaches 145 degrees. Remove from grill and allow rib eyes to stand for about 5 minutes before serving.

For the Salad: Combine all salad ingredients in desired amounts, except for the goat cheese. Mix the dressing and add on top of the salad. Once salad is coated with dressing, gently mix in goat cheese. Portion out onto plates and top with grilled steak.

Succulent Pork Tenderloin Medallions with Black Cherry Marinade

Makes about 4 servings.

Hands down, this is one of my favorite recipes in the book—and my neighbor Alysia agrees!

Marinate overnight for best results.

1½–2 lbs pork tenderloin, cut into
   1 ½–inch medallions

¼ cup olive oil

¼ cup black cherry concentrate (if you
   can't find in store, substitute cherry
   juice)

2 teaspoons fresh rosemary, minced

3 tablespoon vegetable broth (do not
   substitute with vegetable bouillon)

2 tablespoons apple cider vinegar

1 tablespoon honey

1–2 dashes black pepper

metal skewers or 6–8 (12 inch) wood
   skewers soaked in water for about 30
   minutes prior to grilling

Combine olive oil, black cherry concentrate, rosemary, vegetable broth, apple cider vinegar, honey, and black pepper. Pour marinade into medium bowl or resealable bag and add pork tenderloin medallions. Marinate overnight in refrigerator—seriously, no shortcuts! Much better if marinated overnight!

Preheat gas grill on high with lid closed; or if using charcoal grill, prepare for direct heat cooking over hot charcoal.

Prior to grilling, remove the pork tenderloin medallions from the refrigerator and allow to sit at room temperature for about 15 minutes. Place medallions widthwise on metal or soaked wood skewers.

Carefully coat the grill surface with cooking spray, spraying at an angle. Add the pork tenderloin medallions directly over heat. With grill lid open, cook for about 3–4 minutes on one side and turn. After about 3 minutes on second side, check internal temperature. If internal temperature is between 140–145 degrees remove from heat immediately. Remove from grill and allow tenderloins to stand for about 5 minutes before serving.

Great served with grilled rosemary heirloom potatoes cooked in tin foil. See page 144 for the recipe.

Grilling Secret #27
Marinate the meat overnight for an absolute lip-smacking combination of flavors. It doesn't have the same tang from the black cherry concentrate otherwise.

Paleo Burger with Chipotle Aioli

Makes about 4 burgers and about ½ cup of chipotle aioli.

For the burger patties:

about 1 lb ground beef

1 tablespoon garlic, smashed and
  minced

2 tablespoons white or yellow onion,
  minced fine

1 teaspoon dry mustard

2 dashes Worcestershire sauce

1 teaspoon smoked paprika

dash of cayenne pepper

1 egg, beaten

Himalayan pink salt and fresh cracked
  pepper to taste

a dash or 2 of liquid smoke (optional)

For the aioli:

½ cup Vegenaise®

1 teaspoons chipotle powder

½ teaspoon granulated garlic, or garlic
  powder

1 teaspoon whole grain Dijon mustard, or
  dry mustard

salt and pepper

In a medium bowl mix together ground beef, garlic, onion, mustard, Worcestershire sauce, smoked paprika, cayenne, egg, and salt and pepper. Divide meat into 4 equal portions and form into patties.

Grilling the burgers: Preheat gas grill on high with lid closed; or if using charcoal grill, prepare for direct heat cooking over hot charcoal.

Carefully coat the grill surface with cooking spray, spraying at an angle. Add burgers directly over heat and cook for about 3–4 minutes each side. Remove from heat and allow burgers to stand for about 3–4 minutes before serving.

For chipotle aioli: In a small bowl combine Vegenaise®, chipotle powder, granulated garlic, Dijon mustard, salt, and pepper. Mix until ingredients are well combined.

Place burger patties on crisp lettuce and top with chipotle aioli. Garnish burgers with your favorite toppings.

Burger topping options: Grilled onions, sliced tomatoes, grilled mushrooms, avocado, butter lettuce. There are no wrong answers here!

Grilled Rib Eye with Sage Butter

Makes 2 servings.

For the steaks:

2 rib eye steaks, grass-fed preferred
   (or whatever steak cut you enjoy)
drizzle of extra virgin olive oil
2 cloves garlic, minced
Himalayan pink salt and fresh ground
   pepper to taste

For the sage butter:

¼–¾ stick unsalted butter or ghee
4–6 fresh sage leaves (if you can't find
   in store, substitute with 1–2 teaspoons
   rubbed sage leaves)

Grilling the rib eyes:

Drizzle steaks with extra virgin olive oil,
add minced garlic, and sprinkle both
sides with salt and pepper. Let rest out of
the fridge while grill is heated to flavor up
the meat.

Preheat gas grill on high with lid closed; or if using charcoal grill, prepare for direct heat cooking over hot charcoal.

Carefully coat the grill surface with cooking spray, spraying at an angle. Add rib eyes directly over heat. With grill lid open, cook for about 4–5 minutes a side or until internal temperature reaches 145 degrees. Remove from grill and allow rib eyes to stand for about 5 minutes before serving.

For Sage Butter: In small saucepan, melt butter with sage leaves and cook until butter is slightly browned.

Top rib eyes with sage butter when serving.

The Albino Burger (turkey burger)

Makes about 4 servings.

About 1 lb ground turkey

1 egg, whisked

1 teaspoon minced garlic

2 teaspoons minced yellow onion

3 tablespoons breadcrumbs

4–5 fresh sage leaves, finely minced or
   use rubbed sage leaves

⅓ cup grated parmesan or asiago
   cheese

½ teaspoon rosemary, ground

Himalayan pink salt and fresh cracked
   pepper to taste

In a medium bowl, add the whisked egg and mix in all other ingredients, except turkey. Stir well, then add ground turkey and mix thoroughly with your hands. Divide meat into 4 equal portions and form into patties, each about the size of the palm of your hand.

Preheat gas grill on high with lid closed; or if using charcoal grill, prepare for direct heat cooking over hot charcoal.

Carefully coat the grill surface with cooking spray, spraying at an angle. Add burgers directly over heat and cook for about 3–4 minutes a side. Use a thermometer to ensure burgers are at least 160 degrees in the center. Remove from heat and allow burgers to stand for about 5 minutes before serving.

Serve with your favorite toppings!

BBQ Burger Topped with Turkey Bacon

Makes 3–4 servings.

No matter how flavorful the burger is, I do love my condiments! Must be the southern gal in me.

about 1 pound ground beef (I used grass-fed, free-range organic beef)

2 teaspoons granulated garlic (or garlic powder)

1 tablespoon minced white onion

5–6 tablespoons hickory smoked store-bought BBQ sauce

all natural turkey bacon (about 2 slices per burger)

Himalayan pink salt and fresh black pepper to taste

In a medium bowl, mix together ground beef, granulated garlic, onion, hickory smoked BBQ sauce, and salt and pepper with your hands. Divide meat into 4 equal portions and flatten with your hands to form into patties.

Preheat gas grill on high with lid closed; or if using charcoal grill, prepare for direct heat cooking over hot charcoal.

Place turkey bacon on tin foil directly on the grill. Cook for about 2 minutes per side or until crispy.

Carefully coat the grill surface with cooking spray, spraying at an angle. Add burgers directly over heat and cook for about 3–4 minutes on each side. Use a thermometer to ensure burgers are at least 160 degrees in the center. Remove from heat and allow burgers to stand for about 5 minutes before serving. Top with turkey bacon.

Topping options: add ketchup, mustard, or more BBQ sauce.

Serve with Grilled Chipotle Sweet Potato Fries! Check out page 10 for the recipe.

Chapter 8

Seafood and Grill It

Ahi Tuna with Orange & Ginger Miso Marinade

Makes 2 servings.

2 ahi tuna steaks

1 tablespoon miso paste

4 tablespoons lime juice

4 tablespoons orange juice

4 tablespoons coconut sugar or raw
  sugar

1 teaspoon dry ginger

2 teaspoons orange zest

¼ teaspoon cayenne pepper

1 teaspoon minced garlic

Marinating the ahi: In small saucepan, combine miso, lime juice, orange juice, coconut sugar, dry ginger, orange zest, cayenne pepper, and garlic. Cook marinade on medium heat, stirring constantly. Remove from heat once sugar has dissolved. Allow marinade to cool. Pour marinade into medium bowl or resealable bag and add ahi steaks. Mix to coat thoroughly. Marinate in refrigerator for 3–4 hours.

Grilling the Ahi: Prior to grilling, remove the ahi steaks from the refrigerator and allow to sit at room temperature for about 5–10 minutes.

Preheat gas grill on high with lid closed; or if using charcoal grill, prepare for direct heat cooking over hot charcoal.

Carefully coat the grill surface with cooking spray, spraying at an angle. Add the ahi steaks directly over heat. For well-done ahi steaks, cook for about 5 minutes a side or until internal temperature reaches 145 degrees. Remove from grill and allow to stand for about 5 minutes before serving.

Grilling Secret #28

Shown here with black japonica rice, sometimes called "mahogany rice." It has a wonderful nutty taste! You can cook rice directly on the grill using an oven-safe saucepan. Cook rice as you would any other kind of rice: Use 2 parts liquid to 1 part rice, covered and cook directly on grill grate until tender, or about 20 minutes. Note: Because grill temperatures vary, you may need to add a little more water.

Halibut with White Peach Salsa

Makes 2 servings.

3 white peaches, skin on, diced

3 nectarines, skin on, diced *

juice of 4 large limes

4 large garlic cloves, minced

1½ cups of sweet cherry or grape
   tomatoes, cut into quarters

½ jalapeño pepper, seeded and diced

2–4 tablespoons fresh cilantro, diced

1 lb halibut filet

*If nectarines aren't available use total
   of 6 white peaches or any kind of
   peaches

In a bowl combine peaches, nectarines, lime juice, garlic, tomatoes, jalapeño, and cilantro. Allow salsa to sit at least an hour or more so the flavors can mingle. If you make it the day before, it really enhances the flavors!

Preheat gas grill on high with lid closed; or if using charcoal grill, prepare for direct heat cooking over hot charcoal.

Drizzle halibut with extra virgin olive oil and sprinkle with salt and pepper.

Carefully coat the grill surface with cooking spray, spraying at an angle. Add the halibut directly over heat. Cook for about 6 minutes on one side and turn. Cook second side for about 4–5 minutes or until internal temperature reaches 145 degrees. Remove from grill and allow to stand for about 1–3 minutes before serving. Serve "family-style" as shown or cut in half to serve on 2 plates.

Whole Red Snapper with Hoisin Sauce

Makes 4 servings.

It works best to marinate this for at least an hour or more.

1½–2 lbs. whole red snapper, scaled and
dressed

½ cup light soy sauce

1½ tablespoons hoisin sauce

1 teaspoon sesame oil

3 tablespoons coconut sugar (can also
use raw or brown sugar)

1 red Fresno chili, seeded and diced

1 tablespoon fresh ginger, peeled and cut
into strips

1 tablespoon lemongrass paste (or fresh
minced lemongrass)

½ cup finely chopped cilantro (reserve
¼ cup for garnish)

4 cloves garlic, diced

1¼ teaspoon lime zest

In medium saucepan, combine soy sauce, hoisin sauce, sesame oil, coconut sugar, Fresno chili, ginger, lemongrass paste, cilantro, garlic, and lime zest. On medium heat, stirring constantly, heat just until sugar dissolves. Taste to determine if more chile or sugar is needed. Remove from heat and allow to cool.

Place snapper in a 9 x 13-inch casserole dish and add marinade, reserving a little of marinade to drizzle on top after cooking. Place coated fish in refrigerator and let marinate, covered, for at least 1 hour.

Prior to grilling, remove the snapper from the refrigerator and allow to sit at room temperature for about 5–10 minutes.

Preheat gas grill on high with lid closed; or if using charcoal grill, prepare for direct heat cooking over hot charcoal.

Carefully coat the grill surface with cooking spray, spraying at an angle. Add the snapper directly over heat. With grill lid closed, cook for about 6–8 minutes on one side. Use 2 tongs or 2 spatulas to gently turn snapper and cook for another 6–8 minutes on the second side, or until internal temperature reaches 145 degrees. Remove from heat and allow to stand for at least 5 minutes before serving. Serve on large platter. Squeeze fresh lime over the top, sprinkle with remaining cilantro, and garnish with lime wedges. Serve with the marinade that had been set aside.

Option: Serve with fresh fruit slices such as mango or pineapple to complement the spiciness.

Grilling Secret #29
For easier grilling and flipping of the fish, use a stainless steel grill basket or fish basket for the snapper.

Grilled Tiger Shrimp with Lemongrass & Fresno Chili Peppers

Makes 2 servings.

It works best to marinate this for at least an hour.

For the shrimp:

8 tiger shrimp (or 10–12 large shrimp)

¼ cup lime juice

1 teaspoon lime zest

1 tablespoon Fresno chili peppers, seeded and diced

1 tablespoon lemongrass paste

¼ cup fish sauce

3 tablespoons coconut sugar (or raw sugar)

½ cup coconut milk

¼ cup fresh cilantro, diced (recipe option: substitute with fresh Thai basil)

¼ cup fresh mint, diced

2 teaspoons fresh ginger, grated

1 tablespoon garlic, minced

¼ cup rice wine vinegar

2 tablespoons grapeseed oil

For black japonica rice:

1 cup black japonica rice

2 cups water

dash of pink salt and pepper

Combine lime juice, lime zest, chili peppers, lemongrass paste, fish sauce, coconut sugar, coconut milk, cilantro, mint, ginger, garlic, rice wine vinegar, and grapeseed oil. Stir until well mixed and sugar has completely dissolved. Add shrimp to marinade and place in refrigerator while grill is heating.

Preheat gas grill on high with lid closed; or if using charcoal grill, prepare for direct heat cooking over hot charcoal.

Carefully coat the grill surface with cooking spray, spraying at an angle. Remove shrimp from the refrigerator and place directly over heat. With grill lid open, cook for about 2–3 minutes a side or until internal temperature reaches 145 degrees. Remove from heat.

To prepare the rice: In a saucepan, bring water to boil. Add rice, salt and pepper and cook for 1 minute. Reduce, cover, and simmer on low heat for about 20 minutes or until tender.

Serve the grilled shrimp on top of black japonica rice or mahogany rice. Garnish with lime wedges and fresh cilantro, or Thai basil and fresh squeezed lime, if desired.

Note: If using large shrimp rather than tiger shrimp, you may want to use bamboo skewers for easier grilling.

Tuna Melt on a Portobello

Makes 2 servings.
(adapted from a recipe by my friend Kelli Felix)

1 can solid albacore tuna,
    packed in water
1½ tablespoons Vegenaise® or
    mayonnaise
1 teaspoon Dijon mustard (smooth or
    whole grain)
1 teaspoon capers
2 teaspoons green onions, sliced
2 tablespoons breadcrumbs
3 tablespoons fresh garden herbs,
    minced (mix and match, recom-
    mended: flat-leaf parsley, rosemary &
    tarragon, basil)
2 large portobello mushrooms, cleaned,
    with stems removed
lots of fresh cracked pepper
dash of cayenne pepper to taste
dash or two of garlic powder to taste
dash or two of pink salt to taste
grated asiago cheese or a slice of
    Swiss cheese

In medium bowl, combine tuna, Vegenaise®, Dijon mustard, capers, green onions, herbs, breadcrumbs, salt and pepper, and stir until well mixed. With gill side up, fill portobellos with heaping scoops of tuna. Mound tuna mixture generously.

Preheat gas grill on high with lid closed; or if using charcoal grill, prepare for direct heat cooking over hot charcoal.

Carefully coat the grill surface with cooking spray, spraying at an angle. Place filled portobellos directly over heat. With grill lid open, cook for about 3–5 minutes. Place a mound of grated asiago (or slice of Swiss cheese) on top of each portobello and close grill lid for about 1 minute to allow cheese to melt.

Carefully remove from grill with spatula and serve immediately.

Mojito Salmon

Makes about 2 servings.

Marinate the salmon for at least 2 hours for best results.

1 lb salmon filet cut into 2 pieces, if
    desired (or cook it as 1 piece)

1 shallot, peeled and trimmed

¼ cup fresh mint

¾ cup lime juice, fresh is best

1 clove garlic

1 tablespoon lime zest

½ teaspoon mild chili powder

3 tablespoons blue agave nectar or
    honey

2 tablespoons extra virgin olive oil

pink salt and fresh cracked pepper to
    taste

In food processor, combine shallot, mint, lime juice, garlic, chili powder, lime zest, blue agave nectar, extra virgin olive oil, salt, and pepper. Pulse until well mixed. Place salmon in medium bowl or resealable bag and add marinade. Place in refrigerator for 20–30 minutes before grilling.

Preheat gas grill on high with lid closed; or if using charcoal grill, prepare for direct heat cooking over hot charcoal.

Prior to grilling, remove the salmon from the refrigerator and allow to sit at room temperature for about 5 minutes.

Carefully coat the grill surface with cooking spray, spraying at an angle. Add the salmon directly over heat. Cook for about 5 minutes a side or until internal temperature reaches 145 degrees. Remove from grill and allow to stand for about 5 minutes before serving.

Grilling Secret #30
Serve with the Tomatillo Salsa on page 142.
Add more mint to the salsa if desired.

Baltimore Crab Cakes

Makes about 6–8 servings.

16 ounces lump crabmeat, picked
  through for possible shell pieces

⅓ cup Vegenaise® or good quality
  mayonnaise

⅓ cup whole wheat breadcrumbs or good
  quality crackers crumbled

1 tablespoon Dijon mustard (not whole
  grain if you have it)

juice of one whole lemon

1 large egg, beaten

dash of salt and fresh cracked pepper

¾ teaspoon Old Bay Seasoning®

2 tablespoons fresh parsley, chopped
  (optional)

extra lemon wedges for serving

In a large bowl, combine crab meat, Vegenaise®, crumbs, dijon mustard, lemon juice, egg, salt, pepper, Old Bay Seasoning, and parsley, mixing just until combined and being careful not to overwork the crab meat. Shape the mixture into 1½ inch-thick crab cakes and transfer to a wax paper-lined plate or casserole dish. Refrigerate until firm, about 20–30 minutes.

Preheat gas grill on high with lid closed; or if using charcoal grill, prepare for direct heat cooking over hot charcoal.

Carefully coat the grill surface with cooking spray, spraying at an angle. Add the crab cakes directly over heat. Cook for about 5–8 minutes on each side or until internal temperature reaches 145 degrees. Remove from grill and allow to stand for about 5 minutes before serving. Serve with wedges of lemon.

Grilled Scallops with Lemon Tarragon Butter and Greens

Makes about 2 servings.

6–8 large sea scallops

½ stick unsalted butter or ghee softened

1 large clove garlic, smashed and minced

leaves from 3 sprigs (about 6 inches
    in length) of fresh lemon tarragon,
    minced

pink salt and fresh cracked pepper
    to taste

1 lemon cut into wedges

fresh baby kale or baby arugula

4 metal skewers or 12-inch wooden
    bamboo skewers, soaked in water for
    about 20 minutes

In a small saucepan, over medium heat, combine butter, garlic, lemon tarragon, salt, and pepper until butter is melted. Remove from heat and allow to cool to room temperature.

Preheat gas grill on high with lid closed; or if using charcoal grill, prepare for direct heat cooking over hot charcoal.

While grill is heating, place 4 scallops widthwise on each of the pre-soaked bamboo skewers. Generously brush scallops with the lemon tarragon butter. Carefully coat the grill surface with cooking spray, spraying at an angle. Add the scallops directly over heat. Cook for about 3–5 minutes on each side, or until internal temperature reaches 145 degrees.

In a bowl, add baby arugula or baby kale. Add fresh squeezed lemon. Add lemon zest if desired. Add a dash of pink salt and pepper. Plate greens and place scallops on top to serve.

Barramundi with Arugula Pesto

Makes about 2 servings.

2 barramundi filets (or mahi mahi filets)
2–3 tablespoons extra virgin olive oil
salt and pepper to taste

Arugula Pesto

2 cups arugula, chopped (or use 1 cup
  arugula, and 1 cup fresh basil
½ cup walnuts or pine nuts, slightly
  browned
¼ cup Parmesan cheese, grated
2 large garlic cloves, smashed and
  minced
⅓ cup (or less) extra virgin olive oil
dash of fresh cracked pepper

Drizzle filets with extra virgin olive oil and sprinkle with salt and pepper.

Preheat gas grill on high with lid closed; or if using charcoal grill, prepare for direct heat cooking over hot charcoal.

Carefully coat the grill surface with cooking spray, spraying at an angle. Add the filets directly over heat. Cook for about 5 minutes on each side or until internal temperature reaches 145 degrees. Remove from grill and allow to stand for about 5 minutes before serving. Serve with arugula pesto.

Shown here with grilled heirloom carrots and grilled heirloom baby potatoes (pages 138 and 144).

To make the Arugula Pesto: Blend ingredients in food processor until it becomes a paste. Add more or less olive oil to change consistency.

Salmon Plank with Wasabi Aioli and Sweet Soy

Makes 2 servings.
Use a cedar or apple wood plank in this recipe.

This recipe does not require marinating.

1 4–6-ounce fillet of salmon (I used boneless wild caught Keta salmon)

2–3 teaspoons sweet soy* (or regular soy sauce)

2 tablespoons honey, maple syrup, or agave nectar

2 cloves fresh garlic, smashed and minced

fresh cracked black pepper, and sea salt or pink salt as desired

cooking spray (I used coconut oil cooking spray)

Wasabi Aioli

½ cup Vegenaise® or mayonnaise

1 teaspoon wasabi paste (or more to taste)

½ teaspoon rice vinegar (or seasoned rice vinegar) a dash or two of ground ginger (or ¼ teaspoon fresh ginger)

*Sweet soy is a thicker soy sauce that can be found at Asian markets or in the Asian section of grocery store aisle.

Before grilling soak the cedar plank by setting in a sink of water. Place a bowl of water on top of the wood to keep it submerged. The wood should be soaked between 1–3 hours prior to cooking.

Mix all ingredients together and coat the salmon. Set aside.

Preheat grill on high with the lid closed.

Remove the plank from water and dry slightly. Spray both sides with cooking spray and place the plank on the grill with the smooth side up. Allow the wood to heat up for about 5 minutes with the grill closed before adding the fish.

Once the plank is heated, carefully spray the surface with cooking spray and place the filet on the wood skin-side down. Spoon or brush on the sauce and reduce heat slightly to medium-high. Season with salt and pepper. Cover and grill for about 10–15 minutes or until the fish reaches the desired temperature (at least 145 degrees in the thickest part).

Once done, remove plank from grill and place on table with a trivet underneath. Top with wasabi aioli and a bowl of sweet soy for guests to drizzle on. Serve with stir fried brown rice and snow peas with a hint of sweet soy mixed in.

To make the Wasabi Aioli: Mix all ingredients in a bowl. Like it? Use the Wasabi Aioli with the recipe on page 24, too.

Grilled Halibut with Root Veggie Hash

Makes about 2 servings.

For the halibut:

1 or 2 halibut filets, about 2–3 ounces
 each

2–3 tablespoons extra virgin olive oil

Himalayan pink salt and fresh cracked
 pepper to taste

For the root veggie hash:

2–3 carrots, peeled, diced into chunks

2 parsnips, peeled, diced into chunks

1 yam or 2 small sweet potatoes, diced
 into chunks (skins can be left on, if
 desired)

2½ cups vegetable broth

2 cloves garlic

1 cup black japonica rice (or also called
 mahogany rice)

extra virgin olive oil

tin foil

Drizzle filets with extra virgin olive oil and sprinkle with salt and pepper.

Preheat gas grill on high with lid closed; or if using charcoal grill, prepare for direct heat cooking over hot charcoal.

Carefully coat the grill surface with cooking spray, spraying at an angle. Add the filets directly over heat. Cook for about 5 minutes a side or until internal temperature reaches 145 degrees. Remove from grill and allow to stand for about 5 minutes before serving.

Prepare veggie hash: Coat veggies with a little cooking spray. Place in a piece of tin foil and fold to make a pouch. Place directly on the grill, slightly off to the side, and close the lid. Turn once or twice and carefully open up parcel to check if the vegetables have become tender. Once fork tender, remove and set aside.

Bring 2 cups of vegetable broth to a boil in a wide skillet. Add the rice and garlic. Reduce heat, cover, and simmer for about 20 minutes or until tender. Once done, add in the vegetables. Season with salt and pepper, and add more broth if a little more liquid is necessary. Stir and transfer to a plate. Serve with grilled fish on top. Garnish with minced parsley.

Chapter 9

Muffin Tin Grilling and Baking Plus Grilled Desserts

Timbale Egg Cups with Grilled Veggies and Spinach

Makes about 8 muffins.

6 eggs

1½ cups fresh baby spinach, chopped

about 1 cup grilled sweet bell peppers
   (I used red and yellow)

1 cup goat cheese, crumbled

black pepper

sea salt or pink salt

about a teaspoon of Italian seasoning

dash of red pepper flakes or cayenne
   pepper

8 large tortilla wraps (I used Rudi's
   Gluten-Free Tortilla Wraps®)

cooking spray

additional options:

½ cup grilled onion, chopped

½ cup grilled mushrooms

3 tablespoons salsa

Preheat gas grill on high with lid closed; or if using charcoal grill, prepare for direct heat cooking over hot charcoal. If you are using a gas grill, reduce the temperature of the grill to medium-high.

In a bowl, mix all ingredients together, except the tortilla wraps.

Spray muffin tin with cooking spray. Rip the tortilla wraps into wedges and line each muffin cup with several pieces. Pour the egg mixture into each cup about ¾ of the way full.

Spray the top with cooking spray and place directly on the grill. Cover and cook on medium-high heat (about 450 degrees) for about 15–20 minutes or until an inserted toothpick comes out clean and dry.

Once done, allow to cool about 5 minutes before removing from the muffin tin. To remove, take a knife and carefully loosen the egg cups around the edges of the muffin tin.

Note: if the tops of the tortilla wrappers are getting too brown, cover the muffin tin with a loose fitting piece of tin foil.

Corn Bread Mini Loaves with Lemon Zest and Blueberries

Makes 8 servings.

3½ cups Bob's Red Mill® Cornbread Mix

1½ cups milk

2 eggs, beaten

3 tablespoons blue agave nectar or
  honey

1 tablespoon vanilla extract

2 tablespoons lemon juice, fresh

zest of 1 lemon

1 cup fresh blueberries

mini loaf pan (makes 8 mini loaves; can
  also use a muffin tin)

cooking spray

In a medium bowl, combine cornbread mix, milk, eggs, blue agave nectar, vanilla extract, lemon juice, and lemon zest. Stir until well combined. Carefully fold in fresh blueberries. Spray mini loaf pan with cooking spray and fill until about ¾ full.

Preheat gas grill on high with lid closed; or if using charcoal grill, prepare for direct heat cooking over hot charcoal. Place mini loaf pan on grill and, with grill lid closed, cook for about 10–15 minutes, or until a wooden skewer inserted in center of muffins comes out clean. Remove from heat and allow to stand for about 5–6 minutes before serving.

Serve with vanilla nonfat Greek yogurt and berries.

Cardamom Chocolate Cookies with Apricot and Orange Zest

Makes about 12, 4-inch cookies cookies.

1 cup unsalted butter, softened, (or use
 ½ cup unsalted butter, and ½ cup
 coconut oil)

1 ½ cups coconut sugar or raw sugar

2 large eggs

1 teaspoon vanilla extract

2 tablespoons orange zest

1 cup whole wheat flour

1 cup almond meal, or almond flour

¾ cup cocoa powder

1 teaspoon baking powder

½ teaspoon sea salt

3 ½ teaspoons cardamom, ground (white
 or green)

½ teaspoon vanilla

½ cup dried apricots, chopped

1 cup slivered almonds

Optional: add a few drops of orange oil

In large bowl, using electric mixer, cream butter and sugar until light and fluffy. Add eggs, vanilla, and orange zest and mix until well combined. In medium bowl, combine flour, cocoa powder, baking powder, sea salt, and cardamom. Gradually blend flour mixture into creamed butter mixture, being careful not to over mix the dough. Fold in apricots and almonds with a spoon.

Preheat gas grill on high with lid closed; or if using charcoal grill, prepare for direct heat cooking over hot charcoal.

Spray a baking sheet with cooking spray. Drop a dollop of batter for each cookie, leaving room in between for the cookie dough to spread out slightly. Transfer the cookie sheet directly to the grill.

With grill lid closed, cook for about 7–9 minutes. Do not overcook.

Cookies should be soft and puffy when done and will flatten as they cool. Remove from heat and eat!

Note: if you only have 1 cookie sheet, be sure to scrape any bits off and spray again with cooking spray before adding the next batch of dough, otherwise they will stick.

Grilled Pears with Yogurt and Honey

Makes 4 servings.

2 large pears, skin on, cut in half with
　　seeds removed
1 cup plain nonfat Greek yogurt
2 tablespoons orange juice
2 tablespoons honey
¼ teaspoon cinnamon
a few walnut pieces
dried cranberries or cinnamon (optional)

In small bowl, combine yogurt, orange juice, honey, cinnamon, and nutmeg and mix well. Set aside.

Preheat gas grill on high with lid closed; or if using charcoal grill, prepare for direct heat cooking over hot charcoal. Carefully coat the grill surface with cooking spray, spraying at an angle. Or, use grill grate with smaller holes in it if you are using small pears, so they don't fall through into the fire. Spray pear halves with cooking spray and place directly on the grill.

Cook for about 3–4 minutes, turning once. Remove from heat and top with yogurt mixture and walnut pieces.

Grilling Secret #31
Use firm pears so they don't become too soft when grilled.

Grilled Bananas with Vanilla Yogurt, Cocoa Nibs and Pound Cake

Makes about 2–4 servings.

2 medium bananas, sliced

1 cup plain nonfat or Greek yogurt

1 teaspoon vanilla extract

1 teaspoon blue agave nectar or honey
plus some for drizzle

2–4 1-inch thick slices store-bought
pound cake

2 tablespoons unsalted butter, melted

coconut sugar (about 2 teaspoons, or to
taste)

1–2 teaspoon cocoa nibs

In a small bowl, combine yogurt, vanilla extract, and blue agave nectar. Place in refrigerator until bananas and pound cake are done grilling.

Preheat gas grill on high with lid closed; or if using charcoal grill, prepare for direct heat cooking over hot charcoal. Carefully coat the grill surface with cooking spray, spraying at an angle.

Place grill-safe skillet directly over heat and sauté bananas in butter and coconut sugar until caramelized and slightly soft. Spray pound cake slices with cooking spray and place directly over heat, cook for about 1–2 minutes per side. Remove from heat. Place pound cake slices on serving platter. Top with grilled bananas, drizzle with vanilla yogurt mixture, and sprinkle with cocoa nibs.

Spicy Sweet Paprika Almonds

Makes about 2 cups.

1 lb Marcona almonds, raw, preferably
   unsalted

½ teaspoon Guajillo pepper powder (can
   substitute mild or medium chili powder)

1 teaspoon smoked paprika

½ cup coconut sugar

1 tablespoon extra virgin olive oil

1 tablespoon water

dash or two of Himalayan pink salt or any
   kind of salt

Preheat gas grill on high with lid closed; or if using charcoal grill, prepare for direct heat cooking over hot charcoal.

In a grill-safe skillet, combine ingredients and stir until almonds are well coated. With grill lid closed, stirring every minute or so, cook for about 5–6 minutes or until maple syrup has caramelized. Remove from heat and transfer almonds to a parchment paper lined cookie sheet. Let stand for about 10 minutes before serving.

Spicy Grilled Pepita Seed Trail Mix with Goji Berries and Granola

Makes about 4–5 cups.

2 cups raw, unsalted pepita seeds

¼ cup pistachios

1 cup oats

⅓ cup coconut sugar or turbinado sugar

2 tablespoons honey

2 tablespoon butter, ghee, or Earth Balance®

1 teaspoon cayenne pepper, or to taste

3 teaspoons cinnamon

2 tablespoons flax seeds

¼ cup goji berries

¼ cup dried cranberries

¼ cup raisins

salt optional

Preheat gas grill on high with lid closed; or if using charcoal grill, prepare for direct heat cooking over hot charcoal.

In a grill-safe skillet, combine all ingredients except for berries, raisins, and flax seeds. With grill lid closed, opening to stir every minute or so, cook for about 6–8 minutes or until caramelized. Time will vary based on heat of grill. Remove from heat, when ingredients start to look dry. Add flax seeds. Stir, then and transfer to a parchment paper lined cookie sheet. Let stand for about 10 minutes before adding the berries and raisins. Mix well.

Bran Muffins with Super Fruit Berries

Makes about 1 dozen muffins.

1 cup bran cereal

¼ cup milk or almond milk

1 cup unsweetened applesauce

¼ cup unsalted butter, softened or use
   ghee

1 egg

½ cup coconut sugar, or turbinado sugar

1 cup whole wheat flour

2 teaspoons baking powder

½ teaspoon baking soda

½ teaspoon salt

2 teaspoons cinnamon

¼ teaspoon allspice

¼ cup dried mulberries (optional)

½ cup golden raisins, or regular raisins

½ cup goji berries

½ cup pepita seeds (optional)

baking cup liners

In medium bowl, combine bran cereal, almond milk, and applesauce. Let stand for about 5 minutes or until moisture has been absorbed. Add butter and egg and beat well. In separate bowl, combine coconut sugar, whole wheat flour, baking powder, baking soda, salt, spices, and goji berries. Add to bran mixture and stir until combined. Add baking cup liners to muffin tin and fill with batter about ⅔ full.

Grilling the bran muffins: Preheat gas grill on high with lid closed; or if using charcoal grill, prepare for direct heat cooking over hot charcoal. Place muffin tin directly over heat and with grill lid closed, cook for about 20–25 minutes or until a knife inserted in the center comes out clean. Remove from heat and serve immediately.

Mini Grilled Apple Cups with Pear and Cranberry

Makes about 6 servings.

2 large apples, skin on, cored and diced

1–2 pears, skin on, cored and diced

½ cup dried cranberries

½ cup store-bought granola or granola
  cereal

1 teaspoon cinnamon

¼ teaspoon ground ginger

2 tablespoons unsalted butter, melted

4 tablespoons coconut sugar or
  turbinado sugar

ramekins

In a medium bowl, combine all ingredients. Stir until well coated.

Spray ramekins generously with cooking spray. Overfill the ramekins with the filling as it will shrink down when heated

Preheat gas grill on high with lid closed; or if using charcoal grill, prepare for direct heat cooking over hot charcoal. Place ramekins directly over heat and with grill lid closed, cook for about 10–12 minutes or until fruit is tender.

Remove from heat and serve immediately.

Grilling Secret #32
Try adding a dollop of vanilla yogurt on top of pies while still warm, or sprinkle with flax seeds.

Index

Note: Page numbers followed by "b" indicate Grilling Secrets boxes.